PATAKI

TAKI

with Daniel Paisner

VIKING

PATAKI

AN AUTOBIOGRAPHY

Jan 23, 1998

To Carol,

Thanks for all you did for
Education in New York.
With best wishes.

Gy Pataki

VIKING
Published by the Penguin Group
Penguin Putnam Inc., 375 Hudson Street,
New York, New York 10014, U.S.A.
Penguin Books Ltd, 27 Wrights Lane,
London W8 5TZ, England
Penguin Books Australia Ltd, Ringwood,
Victoria, Australia
Penguin Books Canada Ltd, 10 Alcorn Avenue,
Toronto, Ontario, Canada M4V 3B2
Penguin Books (N.Z.) Ltd, 182–190 Wairau Road,
Auckland 10, New Zealand

Penguin Books Ltd, Registered Offices:
Harmondsworth, Middlesex, England

First published in 1998 by Viking Penguin,
a member of Penguin Putnam Inc.

1   3   5   7   9   10   8   6   4   2

Photograph on title page by Mike Grolly. Photograph
on page 6 of insert, third from the
top, by Suzanne Dechillo, *The New York Times*.
All other photographs courtesy of
the Pataki family.

LIBRARY OF CONGRESS CATALOGING-IN-PUBLICATION DATA
Pataki, George E.
Pataki: An autobiography / by George E. Pataki with Daniel Paisner.
p.   cm.
Includes index.
ISBN 0-670-87399-X (alk. paper)
1. Pataki, George E., 1945–   . 2. Governors—New York
(State)—Biography.   3. New York (State)—Politics and
government—1951–   . I. Paisner, Daniel.   II. Title.
F125.3.P38A3   1998   98-9774
974.7043'092—dc21
[B]

This book is printed on acid-free paper.

Printed in the United States of America
Set in Palatino
Designed by Betty Lew

I am proud to dedicate this book to the best family anyone could have: to Libby, for her love, guidance, and friendship, and for putting up with me; to Mom and Dad, for their love and sacrifice, and the values they gave to Lou and to me; to my grandparents, for their courage and wisdom in seeking a new life in a strange new world for their children and grandchildren; to Lou, for paving the way; to my aunts, uncles, cousins, and honorary cousins, who helped us all work together; and, of course, to Emily, Teddy, Ali, and Owen, for giving us the reason and inspiration to keep looking to the future.

Pray for a good harvest, but keep hoeing.

—Pataki family motto

Acknowledgments

My sincere thanks to all those who helped make this book possible: to Dan Paisner, for his tireless efforts and hours of attentive listening; to Ed Hayes, for suggesting the idea of a book in the first place; to Annie O'Sullivan, for helping in so many ways; to all the people at Viking Penguin, for helping me to reflect on how my family's experiences have shaped my political thinking, and for making that thinking into a book; and, most important, to my many friends, who have helped me to have such great opportunities in my life.

Contents

PATAKI

1

November 8, 1994—

4:00 P.M.

DOHERTY," I CALLED OUT. "LET'S GO."
"I'm sick," my key campaign aid moaned. "I think they poisoned me." He handed me his cup of soda. "Taste this," he said; "see if it's Diet Coke."

I grabbed the cup, took a sip, and came away with the unmistakable aftertaste of diet soda. "Yes, it's diet," I said. "No one's poisoning you. How in God's name would anyone know you're a diabetic? It's just nerves."

Of course it was nerves. Tom Doherty—my traveling companion and on-site strategist—my twelve-year-old son, Teddy, and I had just stopped at the McDonald's at Thirty-fourth Street and Tenth Avenue for some fries and sodas. Nothing unusual here, except that it was four o'clock in the afternoon on Tuesday, November 8, 1994. Nothing unusual here either, except in just five hours I would either be the next governor of the state of New York or looking for a job.

"On the other hand," I continued, "if someone did poison you, and you died, and I lost the election, this could be my first case in private practice. I'd make a fortune. Take another swig."

Gallows humor never hurts when it's all on the line.

We hopped back into the campaign Suburban, the half-truck, half-car vehicle that had been our main means of transportation for the past twelve months. We were headed over to Penn Station to catch the homeward-bound commuters on the Long Island Rail Road platforms and make one last impression before the polls closed. It was the last scheduled stop in the biggest battle of my career, and I had to shake a few more hands. Actually, I didn't need to be doing any such thing, but I did need to sway these few dozen commuters as surely as I had to breathe. We were at that final, last-ditch point in a campaign where every vote counts, where every move is magnified beyond its real importance. The hours until the polls close never seem to pass. It is a collection of moments frozen in time, and unlike any other.

As soon as we got back into the car, we heard a WCBS Radio report that had me trailing the Democratic incumbent, Mario Cuomo, by two points, according to a late-afternoon exit poll. The bulletin only added to the sense of urgency.

Penn Station, at just about rush hour, was packed with people heading home for Long Island, and these were the folks we wanted to reach with our last push. We knew Nassau County would be tight, and we were trying to make even the slightest difference, which was about what we could expect. I met my campaign volunteers, armed with posters and ad cards to hand out, and walked into the crowd. "Good to see you. Don't forget to vote," I would say, whenever I couldn't find a hand to shake.

"We really need your help."

"Don't forget to vote."

To me, this was the best time of all. I could have done without my nervousness and the most recent news from the WCBS exit poll, but to be out there at this eleventh hour, meeting people, shaking hands, asking for their help to change New York State . . . well, this was democracy at its purest, at the grass roots. I said the same things over and over, and I'd get back shouts of "Good luck," or "We're with you," or "Howard Stern told me to vote for you." It was astonishing how many professional suburban women mentioned Howard Stern—the out-rageously outspoken New York radio personality who had considered making his own run for governor just a few weeks earlier before drop-ping out and endorsing me—as the reason they were voting for me. So much for logic.

"Great reception," I said, turning to Doherty.

"Not bad," he nodded.

Then I turned to Teddy. He flashed a "thumbs up" sign and a smile, which I could tell was a few watts short of enthusiastic. I knew this wasn't exactly Teddy's favorite thing, to be surrounded by thousands of strangers in a mobbed train station with his father's career in the balance. He would rather have been playing hockey, or tossing a ball with his brother, or doing just about anything else. What twelve-year-old wouldn't? But he was a trouper—just as he, Libby, and all the kids had been the whole way through.

I returned the smile and turned back to Doherty. "Tom," I said, "we're going to win. I can feel it in the crowd."

"Yeah," he replied. "It's great." I didn't know until later that he was lying.

I've met many politicians who refuse to campaign on election day, in the belief that if they haven't gotten their message across by then they're in trouble; but I've also met a few who are out until the last possible minute, on the theory that at the very least it couldn't hurt. That's me. I convince myself that even the slightest turn at the last pos-sible moment could make a big difference, although in truth about the best you can hope for is to persuade a few people to head out to their local polling places who might have otherwise stayed home. Typically, the only thing left undecided, at the very end, is whether to vote at all, but that's reason enough for me; in a battle, you do everything you possibly can to win, for as long as you possibly can, until there is noth-ing left to do.

I had a bit more perspective earlier in the day, and I gave a good deal of it to routine and reflection. Every election day, since my first campaign—for mayor of my hometown, Peekskill, in 1981—I stopped at Chuck and Oley's Rainbow Grill on Central Avenue in Peekskill to share a beer with my father and my friend Vinnie Vesce. It was a routine to soothe the election day jitters. That first race was tight and nerve-racking, and once the polls opened I didn't know what to do with myself. I was running against a popular Democratic incumbent in a traditionally Democratic city, and as the clock began its slow tick I began to stew.

My father—a mailman, farmer, and volunteer firefighter—could see I was on edge. He was even more so. "Come on, Georgie," he said. "Let's go down to Chuck and Oley's for a beer. Get your mind off things."

Chuck and Oley's was my father's favorite bar—a small, dark, nondescript taproom with more character than style—and going there was something to do. My father had a Beck's. He always had a Beck's. I usually drank whatever was on tap, but my father knew what he liked. For the next seven elections—another run for mayor, four runs for the state assembly, a primary race for the state senate, and the ensuing try for the senate seat—he had a Beck's. Each time, we'd raise our glasses and remember where we came from, and then we'd go back to headquarters to learn where we might be headed. Each time, when the results came in on the winning side, our toast at Chuck and Oley's seemed doubly sweet, and it grew into such a marvelous tradition that I often thought it was worth the effort of the entire campaign, just to sit down, with something at stake, and share a beer with my old man.

But my father couldn't join me this time out. It wouldn't have registered for him the way it once had. He was suffering from Alzheimer's disease, and his personality had been reduced to an occasional knowing glance, a smile of recognition, a nod the rest of us could mistake for understanding. It had happened quickly, but these past months had been the worst. It was one of the great sorrows of my life, to see him like this, unable to take care of himself—too sick, even, for my mother to care for him at home. He had been a friendly, sinewy-strong man, with a face etched hard by living outdoors and arms the size of tree trunks from working the farm; but now he spent his days in a nursing home for volunteer firefighters in Hudson, New York, up in Columbia County. His body was a wisp, and his mind was usually elsewhere.

Still, Dad was surely with me in spirit, and I kept the tradition. I cast my own vote with Libby and then went down to Chuck and Oley's with Vinnie, a childhood friend who often joined us for these election day toasts. Before we left, I bought a Beck's for my father and another for myself and took them with me to the helipad behind Peekskill Hospital, where I boarded a chopper for Columbia County with Teddy and Tom Doherty. The helicopter was a luxury we'd used only once before during the campaign, and now I used it to make sure my father and I had our beers, Alzheimer's or no.

He was in his room when we arrived, and I tried to put my visit into context for him. As always since he became sick, I greeted him in Hungarian, the language of his youth; he seemed to understand my Hungarian, poor as it was, better than English, which he spoke fluently. "Dad," I said, "I'm running against Mario Cuomo." I waited for a response. "You never liked him, remember?" Then: "I brought you a beer, the same as always. For luck."

My father looked back at me, and I longed to know what he was thinking. Earlier in the campaign, when I told him I was running for governor, he would sometimes get a thoughtful look that I took to be comprehension. He'd occasionally say things like "Cuomo? He'll be tough!" He'd never been a great fan of Mario Cuomo's, and I wanted him to know I was taking Cuomo on. It was important. At times, my mother swore he knew. She could see it in his eyes, she said. He knew. Maybe he did, but I could never swear to it. There was an election poster on the wall of his room, and the nurses told me he'd sometimes point to it, or see me on television, and say, "That's my boy; that's my son."

He was extremely proud, the nurses said, and I wanted to see it for myself, but his eyes were flat on election day. If he had known once, it no longer seemed to matter.

We sat with him a while, Teddy and I—three generations of Patakis, about to make an impact on the lives of millions of New Yorkers. Or not. Five million people were casting their votes that day, and half of them, more or less, were voting for me, with the more or less marking the difference. It was a long way from 1981, when perhaps 5,000 Peekskill residents were voting in the mayoral election, and we were hoping that half of them, more or less, would be voting for me. I gave my father a sip of the beer, and he took it without knowing why.

"Dad," I finally said, as we were getting ready to leave. "Tonight either I'll be the next governor of New York, or I'll have some time to get the farm up and running again, the way it was."

He said nothing at first, but then a remarkable thing happened. My father turned to me and said, "Georgie, you're going to win. You'll beat Cuomo." One moment, his face was blank; the next, it filled with knowing.

It was a miracle, my mother said when I told her about it later that night, and I believe that's just what it was.

Here again, at this late moment in a campaign, there is a tendency to attach too much significance to insignificant events or indicators, but there was no way to dismiss the great surge of good feeling I felt in my father's room that afternoon. This exchange with Dad was surely significant in a personal sense, but I felt that it had to mean something in the grander scheme as well.

We flew down from Columbia County to Manhattan, where we were met by my advance man, Ed Keegan, in the campaign Suburban. Slipping into that giant car was a little like coming home. In a statewide campaign in a state the size of New York, you spend a lot of time on the road, and the Suburban had quickly become our mobile headquarters. There were phones, all kinds of campaign literature, and day-old newspapers, and White Castle hamburger boxes (a touch from Keegan's roots in the Bronx), and the crumbs of half-eaten muffins and pizza.

We spent a lot of time in the air too, hopping from one upstate town to the next, but I much preferred traveling on the ground. Actually, I hated to fly—I dreaded it, really—but there was no avoiding it. We had to fly, and by election night I'd made a few too many trips in single-engine two-seater planes, through all kinds of weather. On one flight, when even the birds knew enough to stay in their nests, I sat alongside an elderly pilot and clenched my teeth while he steered us through the kind of turbulence that left me bouncing up and down, hitting my head against the ceiling, like in a cartoon. I was feeling faint, as if all the blood had drained from my head. Only after we landed did I realize that the pilot's head undoubtedly was feeling as blank as mine from being smacked around. That was the end of single-pilot flying in my campaign.

On another short hop, from Rochester to Elmira just two nights before election day, I bounced around with Libby and the kids and thought we were all crazy to be up in the air all the time. Mostly I was the crazy one, for bringing my family along. It was bad enough that I was jetting from one rally to the next in the tiniest airplanes I'd ever seen, each one smaller than the one before, but at just this moment I saw no reason to put my family through the ordeal. Libby was pale with the same concern, but the kids didn't even notice the turbulence. Teddy thought it was like an amusement park ride, and he was flopping all over the place, having a grand time. Emily, our oldest, was completely calm. "God is holding this plane in the palm of His hands," she said to her mother with absolute composure, at the bottom end of one sudden dip in altitude.

"Yeah?" Libby shot back, with a firm hold on her armrests and a hold on her anxiety that was somewhat less firm. "Well, what's He on?"

The campaign also took us to the rails, when a train ride seemed like a good idea, and to one memorable ferry ride across New York harbor, just days before the election. We were headed to a Sunday night fund-raiser on Staten Island that Borough President Guy Molinari, a great supporter, had arranged, and I was hit full in the face by what all of this meant—my running for governor. I looked out across the water and saw the Statue of Liberty all lit up and shining down on us, and I thought of my grandparents, all four of them passing beneath the great lady to Ellis Island under entirely different circumstances, so many years ago: my father's parents from Hungary; my mother's from Italy and Ireland; all of them desperate for a future they could build for themselves.

God, for my grandparents to know and taste and feel what their journeys had become! I stood by myself, at the ferry's railing, and wondered at the space between us. My grandparents arrived on these shores without knowing the language, with only a few dollars in their pockets, with no plan other than to work hard and provide for their families. And here I was, their grandson, carrying their hope (and their name!) and with a real chance to be the governor of their adopted state. Teddy Roosevelt! Charles Evans Hughes! Franklin Roosevelt! Averell Harriman! Nelson Rockefeller! George Pataki? This was an America they would have been proud of. It was truly astonishing and life-affirming.

Indeed, it was one of the more personal moments of the campaign, and it caught me by surprise; earlier that same Sunday, I hadn't been thinking of family, or legacy, or fate; I'd been focused on the numbers. A *Daily News* poll that morning had me trailing Governor Cuomo by sixteen points—an impossible gap to make up with so little time. I never cared much for all the polling surrounding our campaign, and I never trusted the numbers, but it would have been foolish to disregard a double-digit dip in the polls this close to the election.

I reflected on the same waters that had carried my grandparents to Ellis Island nearly ninety years earlier. It was a remarkable connection, about to be tested. In coming to America, they had placed their whole lives on the line; for me, it was just my political career. I had yet to lose a race, but these latest polls were telling me that my run might be up. I wasn't through, but I might have to sit it out and wait for the next shot. That's politics, right?

Well, not really. Not for me. Sometimes you win, sometimes you lose, and yes, there is always another campaign, but I didn't feel this way. Looking out at the magnificent city lights, I started to realize that

I had to win *this* race, *this* year, *this* time. Not just for me. Not just to win. But to truly change New York, to give the people back their jobs and their hope and confidence in our shared future. I honestly thought that after four more years of Mario Cuomo's failed policies my kids would wind up raising their families in North Carolina, Texas, or Atlanta . . . somewhere other than the state I loved. We *had* to win.

Still, whatever happened in the race for governor, my experience had confirmed the lives my grandparents had made. I was a mailman's son, raised on a small European-style farm on the outskirts of New York City, surrounded by dozens of aunts and uncles and cousins and blessed with the kind of upbringing that had brought me to this time and place. I was taught to believe in hard work, education, and family. I was taught to believe in human resourcefulness, in the limitless possibilities of human beings, and I needed to look no further than our own farm for validation. It was because of those beliefs that I was out there in New York harbor, ferrying to my own fund-raiser, hoping to be the next governor of the greatest state in the country.

And now, on election day, those roots reached to Penn Station, and I walked that Long Island Rail Road platform with a clear goal in mind and a firm sense of where I'd been. I knew that in three or four hours my course would be determined—and so too would the path of all New Yorkers. I'd continue shaking hands and reaching out to as many people as I could, but at this moment I honestly thought I'd win. I took the pulse of those commuters on their way home after work and put myself over the top. I could see it in their eyes and feel it in their grip. I didn't need to look at any numbers. There was an energy in that station that seemed to flow toward me. Of this I was all but certain, because in politics you can never be too sure. Even in certainty, you just never know. If I stopped to think about it, instead of just feeling it, the only thing I would have been sure of was that we had run the right race, for the right reasons, and it all flowed from who I was and what I hoped for. It all went back to my childhood, to my parents, and to their parents before them.

It all went back to the Hudson Valley farm . . . where I come from.

2

Land and Work

I GREW UP ON A FARM. IT WAS JUST OVER A DOZEN ROCKY acres, forty-five minutes by train from New York City, but in my memory it was as pastoral as anything out of Thomas Hardy.

I can still hear the sound of the place: my grandfather, out in the grapevines, working his hoe to a steady beat. *Ka-chunk! Ka-chunk! Ka-chunk!* He would work a hoe until its edge was blunt and rounded from the effort. When I was a boy, I woke to the sound of my grandfather's hoeing most mornings and fell asleep to it most nights. It was the rhythmic sound of steel against earth (or, just as likely, rock): persistent, purposeful, confident. It was the metronome of my growing up, a constant assertion of our place on the land, the cadence of our being there.

The land was in Peekskill, just thirty-five miles north of New York City, on the threshold of the Hudson Highlands—one of the most beautiful places on earth, and a great place to live and work, although the hard joke was that each year our best crop was rocks. Every spring, with each new row we planted, a new crop of rocks pushed up by winter's frost would litter the field, leaving us with new material to put on top of the majestic stone walls surrounding the fields.

It took a lot to get a little, but we farmed every last inch of that land. We even put the swampy part to use, as a pasture for the cows. As a child—in school, when I finally read Thomas Hardy—I used to think of our farm as a scaled-down version of a grand, self-contained manor, because so much of what we ate we grew ourselves; but as an adult I began to recognize that the grandest thing about it was the way our pride of work and of ownership allowed us the pride of doing. Ours was subsistence farming with a frayed blue collar: what we had, we ate; what we had in plenty, we sold; what we needed, we sometimes did without. There were long days and quiet nights, and there was a shared purpose that others, sadly, have rarely known. There was family. There was the belief, always, that tomorrow would be better.

This, to me, was everything. True, family and purpose wouldn't necessarily feed us, but we also had cows and chickens and fruit trees and grapevines and all kinds of fresh vegetables. There was a rickety old cider press, and a corncrib fashioned after the ones in my grandfather's tiny Hungarian village. Corn was one of the staples of the Hudson Valley, and ours was wonderful. We picked it fresh before sunrise, still wet and cold from the dew. Actually, you don't pick corn so much as you break it—two ears at a time, if you're good—and my grandfather had me out there doing just that by the time I was ten.

Ah, there was nothing like the sweetness of an ear of our corn— fresh off the stalk and soft enough to eat without cooking—especially when you were worn out from a full morning of picking. And it wasn't just the corn. I have never eaten, nor will I ever eat, a peach as good as one of my grandfather's Hale Havens or Elbertas; I have never eaten a better tomato or strawberry. My grandfather had high standards, and he passed them on to my father, who in turn passed them on down to the rest of us. But I've often thought that what made our fruits and vegetables so special was that I could taste in them the pride and effort of my entire family. The produce tasted great because I had a hand in it, because we all had a hand in it.

It was, in virtually every aspect, a magical and wonderful childhood. Yes, in economic terms, we may have been poor—the kind of poverty that didn't realize the Depression was over—but we had everything we needed. I thought everyone lived this way, though today I can measure other people's lives and childhood stories against my wistful memories and come up grateful. The contrast between how it was for me then and how it is for me now is startling to many of the people I've met since I've entered public life, but in my head, there is a clear line from the way I was raised to what I became, from the values I was taught to the ones I still hold dear.

My whole world was on that farm. There were my parents, my brother Lou and I, both sets of grandparents, nine aunts and uncles, and twelve cousins—enough, certainly, to keep things interesting. It was a rambling extended-family compound, with the twenty-nine of us living in six different houses dotting various corners and edges of the farm. The center of our lives was the home of my paternal grandparents, and it wasn't much. The old farmhouse dated back to the 1780s, and it was little more than a shack—just a kitchen and two small bedrooms dug into the side of one of the Hudson Highlands' many hills. Grandpa's thinking was that they all spent so much of their time outdoors, working, that they didn't need anything bigger. My father shared the bedroom with three brothers and a sister (with the four boys all in one bed!); when my aunt Zelma was a teenager, Grandpa built a small parlor so that she could receive callers. This parlor was the only room squared with carpenters' tools, because by this time Grandpa and his Hungarian friends had built a few of each other's houses and actually knew what they were doing.

The house I grew up in was just 200 feet to the east of my grandparents' house, separated by a dozen or so rows of grapevines and a big plum tree. My cousin Bobby's house was about 250 feet to the west, on the other side of the grapevines. This, to me, was the triangle of civilization. The original house was without plumbing or heating, except for a wood-burning stove in the kitchen; an outhouse stood as the sole bathroom; but what I remember best was the dirt floor of the cellar, dug into the side of the hill, where every year barrels of homemade wine would be lined up and bubbling. We grew our grapes for only one purpose—wine for the family—and each fall gave over the entire cellar (and most of the porch!) to winemaking.

The winemaking was a full-family effort. We picked the grapes ourselves; this usually took about a week, depending on how many of us were around to help. Then we'd take turns grinding the grapes, which we'd leave to ferment in large oak barrels on the porch before stirring up the juice and pressing it and adding sugar. That was the only concession to the rockpile on which we farmed. We simply could not get the desired sugar content into our grapes from the rugged New York soil (or the limited sun, or the bitter cold), so we added the sugar afterward.

Some years, we made wine from elderberries or gooseberries, very much in the Hungarian tradition. Grandpa could make wine from anything—plums, pears, berries—and to him nobody else's wine tasted as good. We probably made 300 or 400 gallons of the Pataki vintage each fall, and every last drop was gone by the next harvest.

People often think in romantic terms of farms and farmers, as somehow removed from mainstream life. In many ways, they're right. But romanticism aside, a real farmer can't afford to lose focus or perspective. It's a different, often difficult way of life, and yet it teaches a great many lessons. Above all, family farming teaches you to be real. You can't fake it or do a job halfway. You can't weed just half a patch or plant half a field. When a field is ready to be picked, it must be picked—all of it, right away—or the crops will rot, after months of hard work. You don't keep time. You don't keep score. You don't punch out at five o'clock. You just get the job done. If it means watering at midnight, or picking apples at first light in the morning before a storm, you get it done. You don't just slap a new coat of paint on something and hope for the best, because sooner or later it will fall apart. Also, you need to take a long view. You can't simply do a job and be done with it. You have to plan for the next year and the year after that and the year after that. The crop you plant one season has everything to do with what you'll plant the next season, and with what you've planted in seasons past. If you're putting in a tree, you have to plan for twenty years. If you're putting in a grapevine, you have to plan for ten. There are no quick fixes that time, or nature, or plain old bad fortune won't quickly reveal.

If Grandpa had run his farm the way some of my colleagues approached the business of government, his fields would have been barren. You didn't have to look hard to see that the truths I learned while growing up were nowhere apparent in state government. Our state budgets, for example, were consistently late and overburdened with padded items meant to buy support. The padding I could understand—politicians like to say yes, particularly to interests with a lot of power—but the lateness was beyond me. It still is. If the law says that the budget has to be in place by April 1st, then the budget should be in place by April 1st; and yet when I started out in Albany in the mid-seventies the tradition was to stop the clock at 11:59 P.M. and work all night until negotiations were through. Four or five hours later, with a budget finally done, they'd restart the clock and everyone would cheer; and I contented myself with the thought that they were at least upholding the spirit of the law, if not the letter.

But then, one year, someone forgot to stop the clock. Nothing happened. The next year the session went on until April 3rd, and still nothing happened; and eventually it dawned on these presumably well meaning legislators that if they were empowered to make the law, they were also empowered to break it. This is a dangerous notion, and one of its more benign side effects was that each year April 1st passed with less and less notice. April 1st went from being a deadline to being a guideline, and now it's hardly even that. The idea is, *Well, sometime this spring maybe we'll have a budget—if not by spring, then certainly by summer.*

During my first year as governor, I knew I had to do something dramatic—some might say drastic—to get a budget adopted at all, let alone on time. I had promised to cut taxes by $1 billion in 1995, not anticipating Mario Cuomo's departing gift to the people of New York of a $5 billion deficit in that same fiscal year. Many of my advisers said we had to put off the tax cut, maybe even raise taxes to deal with the deficit. Not a chance! That was precisely what had created all the growing cynicism toward politics, and certainly politicians themselves. Promise something in October. Come January, it's "Oh, sorry, things have changed." Well, things had changed—a $5 billion deficit was nothing to sneeze at, but I was going to keep my word.

My proposed budget and its cuts alienated every interest group, every labor union, certainly every reporter, and probably every legislator from both parties. This wasn't the way New York was supposed to work—or rather, this wasn't the way New York's government had operated in the past. Pickets followed me from one end of the state to the other. They picketed the Capitol, my New York City office, our house—it was democracy in action. While my opponents didn't understand, it was all about plowing the fields and planting the trees so we'd have a crop this year, and the next, and the year after that.

So forget about a budget April 1st. How do I get a budget at all? I had a solution, one Jim Tedisco and I had dreamed up when we were in the assembly, trying to stir things up. I simply would refuse to pay myself, other statewide officials, or any legislator until the budget was finally passed. "Governor, are you crazy?" was the restrained response from one of my legislative aides.

"You're a complete nut" was a relatively frequent greeting in the Capitol halls.

"George, you're only causing resentment and delaying the budget," ran another argument. "No one will pass a budget with this gun to his head."

"We'll see," I said. April came. And went. No budget. May came. And went. No budget. They sued. A handful of Democrats from the assembly said I was exceeding my constitutional authority. They won, but I appealed the decision. Still no pay. My appeal stayed the court's decision. June came. No budget. Finally, June 18th—a great budget! We cut spending from the prior year for the first time in fifty-two years. After two and a half months, we achieved historic change. We cut almost $6 billion from the previous budget and put in place a three-year tax cut that has made New York number one in cutting taxes in each of those three years. We did things right. We laid the foundation for the next year, and the year after that. We brought the lessons of discipline every family farmer knows are needed to survive the government of New York State.

As it turned out, the 1995 budget was the earliest on my watch. In 1996, we reached into July, breaking Mario Cuomo's dubious record for the latest budget in state history; and in 1997, we pushed into the middle of August, making our budget the latest ever in the country. Other states don't have these problems, but other states didn't need the magnitude of change necessary to get New York back on track. And while these fights took a long time, they were necessary and resulted in positive change. And other states don't have legislators like the assembly's Democratic leadership, nostalgic for the era of big government, opposed to change, and willing to spin the wheels of government until they all but fall off. Almost everywhere else in the country, the process seems to make sense.

Nothing is certain, in farming or in politics, but back on the farm we at least tried to keep our efforts rooted in something real. Things made sense. The work we did had everything to do with the results we achieved, and these lessons continued to resonate for me even as the backward logic of government continued to astound me. One of the most enduring lessons was passed on to me by my father, by example. Every year until well after my grandfather died, Dad persisted in planting his tomatoes in early April, a good six or eight weeks before anyone else in the Hudson Valley. The thing about tomatoes is that they're especially susceptible to an early killing frost; and in the highlands in April, there is almost always an early killing frost. That was the way of the land and the region. We all thought it was questionable, to work so hard to put the tomatoes in so early, year after year, but Dad was stubborn, and of course we followed his plan. He was determined that one year the tomatoes would make it through and we would be able to sell them a month ahead of anyone else. That was the upside. The downside was our sweat and effort, but we Patakis had these in ready supply. Each night I'd anxiously turn on the television to see the overnight weather forecast—"scattered clouds," "low in the 40s," all good news. But inevitably one night would check in clear with lows in the 20s, and I knew the tomatoes would never make it through. My father and I would spend half the night covering every plant with baskets and plastic, hoping they would keep frost from actually forming on the plants. But it just didn't work. The next morning would come and the plants would be dead. Nevertheless, this mulish ritual had a point: It always pays to reach, to buck the odds, to leave conventional wisdom to the conventional, because in so doing you leave room for hope and possibility.

My grandfather's credo was simple: You have to work. And we did. All of us. Janos Pataki saw to that. He had been born in the tiny Hungarian village of Aranyosapati, a village so small that it didn't appear on most maps. Aranyosapati was in the province of Szabolcs, in the Carpathian basin, and the strength of the people of that region was very much a part of my grandfather. I remember him as proud, dignified, and incredibly powerful. He was short and stocky, with a large square face, thick shoulders, and the brightest blue eyes. Along with my father, he was perhaps the most formidable influence of my childhood. He died when I was a young man, but he is with me still.

Just ask any Hungarian and he'll tell you, "Hungarians are unique." Ask someone else and you'll probably get a diatribe about the "mad Hungarians." In fact, the history of the people of Hungary, the Magyars, is unique and fascinating, and "characters" is an inadequate term to describe them.

The Magyars first conquered the Carpathian Basin, which became their homeland, in the ninth century, under their king, Arpad. They crossed the Carpathians through a pass just above my grandparents' home village—the traditional invasion route for tribes crossing the steppes of Russia into Europe. The Magyars were not Slavs; they were unrelated to the predominant Russian, Ukrainian, Czech, Slovak, Serb, Croatian, Polish, or other Eastern European peoples of Slavic origins, and the history of their earliest years is lost. But they followed the traditional route of Attila, the Bulgars, and others, and "conquered" their nation in 896.

My grandfather's home region, Szabolcs, was named after the

royal prince left by King Arpad to guard the Carpathian passes; the Szabolcs people were one of the eight tribes of the Magyars. The following centuries proved the wisdom of guarding the back door against invasion, as successive attacks by Cumans, Pechenegs, Mongols, and Russians all sought to use those passes to force their way in to conquer Hungary.

In addition to a tradition of fierce independence, a tradition upheld in later wars against the Turks and Austrians, wars in which only this small part of Hungary and Transylvania retained its independence, was a sense of common purpose. By the end of the eighteenth century, the population of rural Hungary had evolved into three classes—the rich barons, who held vast estates; other large landholders; and small farmers, owners of family land that had been continually divided over the centuries, creating a surplus of rural labor—free, proud, and independent, but desperately poor and in need of new opportunities.

My grandmother's family, the Szoniczs, fell into the second class. Her warrior ancestors were in fact elevated to the nobiity in 1618 for their heroic and successful efforts against the Turks. My grandfather's family, the Patakis, were small landowners. They had a modest family farm but too many strong, healthy children to live off its output.

What they lacked in opportunity, they made up for in work. Grandpa worked all day long, all year long, for as long as he lived. He hated it when people sat around and talked. He had an expression—*Tul szok bezehl!*, "too much talk"—and it rang across his fields like a warning shot.

"Why are you talking," he always said, "when you should be working?"

Despite his not talking, he found time to tell me a few things. If we were working, side by side, it was sometimes okay to talk. Talking made the time pass and drew us together. He used to tell me how he'd had to sleep in churchyards when he was ten or eleven years old. Both his parents had died when he was young—his father after taking sick in a fall through ice on the Tisza River, which ran from Transylvania into Hungary proper. He had no place to live. When he finally moved in with an uncle, he was made to sleep in the barn with the animals. He never forgot that, and he wanted his grandchildren to remember it as well.

In a very poor corner of a very poor country, he still had it tougher than most people. He was so poor, he used to tell me, and the countryside so fertile, that if he found a rare rock in the soil he would put it in his pocket and keep it to sharpen his few tools. And yet somehow this penniless orphan managed to win the affection of the woman who would be my grandmother, Erzabet Szonicz, a beauty from a prominent local family. In the eyes of my grandmother's family, it was not exactly a match made in heaven. They were a noble family at the top of the ladder in Aranyosapati, and my grandfather was on the bottom rung; but he was extremely handsome, a fine singer, and a gentleman, and he and Erzabet fell in love. He was Roman Catholic, she was a Greek Catholic, the religion of the upper class, combining Catholic theology with Greek ritual. After such a mismatch in standing and station, there was nothing to do but make for America and a better life on equal footing.

My grandparents got off to a slow start. There was enough money only for my grandfather's passage. He left my grandmother behind with their infant son, my uncle John, hoping to send for them as soon as possible. This was the way for many immigrants around the turn of the century, and on through the Second World War, and my grandfather followed the path of hundreds of Hungarians to Peekskill. He arrived at Ellis Island on September 10, 1905, at the age of twenty-seven. He had his life savings, eleven dollars, in his pocket.

Grandpa found grueling work at the Peekskill Hat Factory, on North Division Street, along with hundreds of other Hungarian immigrants. His job was to dip the felt in mercury and then in dye, six days a week, ten hours a day, for one dollar per week. His hands were stained from the dye for the rest of his life, but he was able to save enough to arrange passage for his family two years later. It was a terrible job—tedious, toxic, low-paying—but he didn't speak any English, and his opportunities were few. There was the Baker Underwear Factory, and the Fleischmann's yeast plant, and the hat shop, which had been magnets for the first wave of Hungarian immigrants, about 1895. Grandpa had known a handful of family friends from his village who were already working at the hat shop, so they helped him get established there.

My grandmother had her own version of our family history, and she told it often. One of her favorite refrains was a line from her own mother, who sent her off to America—and to a husband beneath her station—with the following advice: "Let people help you to carry your bags," her mother said, "but never let anybody hold your baby." Grandma arrived at Ellis Island on December 19, 1907, with my uncle John in her arms and a crudely lettered cardboard sign marked "Peekskill." She never got over the fact that she was able to find her way to Grand Central Station and onto the right train to meet my grandfather without knowing the language. The sign was enough. Everyone was just so friendly, my grandmother recalled fondly, leading her to the door of her house, helping her with her luggage, even offering to carry the baby. I often think of her when I see someone obviously new to our country standing at a station or on a corner, and I try to return the favor. She had fallen in love with America, and Americans, from the start. Still, she never once let go of my uncle until she was safely inside her new home.

That new home wasn't much. My grandparents lived in workers' housing, and later on with friends, doubling up with other families when space and money were short. There were about 500 jobs at the hat factory, at peak operation, and there was not enough housing to go around; but most of the workers were Hungarian—most of them from the same area of Szabolcs—so people helped each other out. Many workers lived dormitory-style, in boardinghouses built for several families. That's what my grandparents did when they were just starting out, sharing the cooking and cleaning and other chores with the other families.

It was an extremely insular community: Hungary, once removed.

Visitors to one of these factory boardinghouses might never have known they were in America. People almost never spoke English—only when they had to, and then haltingly. What little social activity there was took place around the local Hungarian church, which soon became home, also, to a burgeoning Hungarian-Jewish population. This was America, without the restrictions and structures of the Old World. The church functioned not only as a religious center but also as a cultural and ethnic tie, and there was room for everybody.

My father was born in Peekskill but couldn't speak one word of English until he started public school at the age of six—at Uriah Hill, an elementary school at the north end of town built in part with money donated by Peekskill's civic-minded Hungarian-Americans. It's where I went to school, and where my own children started out. I can't tell you the tremendous sense of pride I felt the first day I walked our daughter to the same school my grandfather and his friends had helped to build, to the school where my father learned English, to the site of so many of my own childhood memories . . . all of this dating to a time when there was barely enough to keep our family fed and warm in winter.

Education was important to that first wave of Hungarian immigrants. If there was ever a question of studying versus working, my father was told to study, even when it was time to pick. My grandfather may have had high standards for his peaches and tomatoes, but he had even higher standards for his children. They were expected to do well in school. As with farming, it wasn't just going through the motions. The children were in school for a reason: to lay a foundation for a better life; there was honor in hard work, and in sweat, but only if work and sweat dovetailed with the pursuit of knowledge.

That's how it was for all of us cousins, too. By the time we reached school age, we'd been taught to expect the best of ourselves. We were given both the discipline of work and the love of learning, and these were handed down by example. My older brother, Louis, was the famous reader in our family, and I basically read what he read, four years later. When I was about eight or nine, my mother gave me a subscription to the Landmark Book Club, and I used to devour each month's selection the day it arrived in the mail. Biography, history, science . . . I loved it all. Of course, I eagerly looked forward to my monthly subscription to Walt Disney's Comics and Stories, which my aunt Helen had given me at around the same time, and I tore into those as well, as each new issue arrived. The comics never arrived the same day as the books, so I never had to reveal a preference, but I suppose I would have reached first for the comics. I still have all those old comics.

Back in Hungary, reading hadn't been any kind of ticket to a different way of life. Reading wasn't anything at all. When I went back to Hungary as an adult, I could see that the influences of the modern age have hardly dented the centuries-old customs of my grandfather's small village. It's very stratified, and people rarely change their status or their family occupations. You are born into a way of life, and that's how it is until you die; opportunity doesn't find you, because it doesn't know where to look. In rural Hungary—unlike America—education wasn't a way up and out.

But my grandfather wasn't one to be limited by the boundaries or the traditions of his village, and once he married my grandmother it was clear he couldn't follow his predetermined course. Even before they were married, he was always striving to achieve, to improve his situation. That was the nature of most immigrant Americans, people like my grandfather who were willing to risk everything in hope of a better life, understanding that there were no guarantees but that the better life would begin with the education of their children.

And so it did for Janos Pataki and his family. Predictably, that better life didn't come to him, and it certainly didn't reach inside the sweltering walls of Peekskill's hat factory. In fact, my grandfather eventually raised his voice to protest the hideous working conditions there. The mercury fumes were said to invade the nervous system and leave men shaking and uncertain; the expression "mad as a hatter" and Lewis Carroll's character the Mad Hatter came from the peculiar behavior—due to mercury poisoning—of longtime workers in British hat factories. My grandfather didn't show any effects beyond the stains on his hands; still, it was a terrible place to work, and I was always proudest of Grandpa when listening to stories of his experience in the hat factory. He wasn't trained to do any other kind of work, except farming; but he was never one to sidestep a fight, and he took the lead in this one, along with a few others, in a bitter dispute that divided the community and cost hundreds of breadwinners their jobs.

I never pressed my grandfather on how he came to such a leadership position, but I suspected it had to do with the fact that by 1923, when the mostly Hungarian workforce succeeded in shutting down the factory, his English had become a little better than that of most of his coworkers (thanks, probably, to his abiding interest in the American schoolwork of his young children), and that he was a little more passionate about what he believed in. Whatever it was, he wound up at the forefront of a labor strike against the factory, which was itself remarkable. At this time, the organized labor movement was in its infancy, and immigrant workers were loath to put their meager paychecks and prospects at risk; but everybody had a breaking point.

I doubt if it was a coincidence that about the same time, the strike at Andrew Carnegie's Homestead Mill in western Pennsylvania was taking place. Nor was it a coincidence that that strike, too, was led by immigrants from Hungary. A history of independence is a hard thing to break. Indeed, at around the time my grandfather left Hungary, the country was felled by the most crippling labor strike in its history, when 3,000 mine workers lifted their pickaxes to protest the pitiful wages and horrendous working conditions there. Unlike previous labor strikes, which had usually lasted just a few hours, this one was well organized in my grandfather's home region of Szabolcs and succeeded in halting trade on the Danube and winning temporary reforms. It was clear that the uprising back home had in some ways informed the walkout at the hat factory in Peekskill; at the very least, it helped to feed the huge wave of Hungarian immigration to this country. Surely, many of Grandpa's coworkers and friends and relatives took part in the mine strike.

There was a place called Gyetko's Bar, at the bottom of Frost Lane, not far from the land we would someday farm, and that was where all the union organizers from the hat factory used to meet, to discuss strategy. Really, there wasn't much to discuss. It was the tail end of the First World War, and labor was up against it; workers could either take things as they were or jeopardize the well-being of their families; the factory was threatening to pull out of town and open shop elsewhere if the union didn't drop its demands and return to the fold. This was a difficult time to stand up for what you believed, if what you believed had to do with fair pay and improved working conditions. Laws protecting those seeking to protest were a far-off future dream. Violence and other tactics to intimidate were real. Leading workers were offered large cash payments to convince others to cross the line. Those who struck had everything to lose and nothing to fall back on, and yet they held to what they believed was right.

In the end, management could not break the union in Peekskill. The factory relocated—without the union—to Danbury, Connecticut; and my grandfather learned one of the hard truths of American business: Principles alone will not put food on the table. Workers' solidarity was not what it had appeared during those late-night organizing sessions at Gyetko's; and to the extent that solidarity did exist, it did not appear to matter. A great many workers decamped with the factory, depleting Peekskill's Hungarian community, splintering many families, and alienating many friends. My grandfather was left without a job or a place to live.

It was, Grandpa remembered, a difficult time, made more difficult by the needs of his expanding family, which now numbered five children and included my father, Louis, born in 1914. Luckily, my grandfather quickly found a job at the Fleischmann's plant at the south end of town, where they made yeast for the company's gin, whiskey, and vodka. At the time, it was the largest yeast factory in the world, and possibly the smelliest. The fermenting molasses drifted up and filled the air with a distinctive, wet aroma that was nearly overwhelming. Inside the factory, it was even worse, a detail I came to know for myself when I took a job there as a teenager. I can still taste it, back on the inside of my throat; my eyes would water just when I thought about the smell—that's how intense it was. I grew used it, after a while (I had to!) but if I came across that smell today it would take me back in a beat.

With the hat factory gone, it seemed that everyone in Peekskill now worked at Fleischmann's. It was the biggest plant in town, with more than 1,000 employees, though very few Hungarians and even fewer refugees from the hat factory. There was a lot of work, but it was hard to get hired if the foremen knew you were one of the workers who had made trouble at the hat factory. Their stained hands gave the hat factory workers away, and the people at Fleischmann's knew that the only employees who hadn't followed the hat factory to Connecticut were the ones who had fought for workers' rights, and they didn't want them around causing any trouble. My grandfather was turned down time and again, because of his hands.

Ultimately, though, he was able to hire on. As Grandpa's story went, he became friendly with some of the workers at Fleischmann's and showed himself proficient at some sport (he never mentioned what sport it was), and they wanted him on the company team. He really wasn't an athlete, in American terms, although he was strong and fearless. He was a great swimmer. As a boy, he swam in the Tisza all the time, and his new friends at the Fleischmann's factory heard him bragging one afternoon about his swimming. He said he could swim across the Hudson, and they got a bet together and put up a keg of beer against my grandfather's claim, and he went out and swam across the Hudson as if it were nothing at all. The river was over a mile wide where the factory stood, and the currents were fairly strong, so this was no small feat.

Grandpa called Fleischmann's the "Yankee factory," because it was where all the Yankees worked. The Yankees, to him, were Protestants, Germans, Irish, or anyone who wasn't eastern or southern European, and most of them didn't like to work alongside Hungarians. This was ironic, because the Fleischmanns themselves were of Hungarian descent, from a village outside Budapest. Grandpa primarily worked the coal cars, where he soon recognized that he was being unfairly treated by a few of his "Yankee" colleagues. At the hat factory, management had been the enemy, but here it could be the man next to him on the line. On certain days, Grandpa would have to shovel out the whole car while his "Yankee" partner sat back and watched the Hungarian do all the work, and after a few years—years when he saved virtually every nickel he made by living in worker housing near the molasses tanks—my grandfather again found himself at his breaking point. It wasn't just one man riding him this way, but a whole group. Grandpa finally got into a fight with one of them, which he won, after which the tension between the mostly German crew and the few Hungarians no longer mattered, because my grandfather was once again out of a job.

This time, he had enough money saved to buy a small piece of dormant farmland, with basically nothing on it but suspect soil and an eighteenth-century farmhouse dug into a hill. The land hadn't been farmed for decades, and the farmhouse hadn't been lived in for years, but Grandpa didn't let this bother him. To own his own land, to control his fate, to not have to answer to anything but the elements, to make his living off the soil and his own effort . . . these had been his quietly held dreams ever since he'd left Hungary. In Hungary, it would have been impossible for him to work and save and buy his own farm. But this was America, and Grandpa was determined. It wasn't clear that he'd ever make any money from the farm, or even that he'd be able to grow enough to support his family, but it was all he could afford. The important thing was it would be *his* land. He was always reaching, struggling for a better way of life for his family. It was this kind of reaching, perhaps, that made my father plant tomatoes every April.

And so by 1925 my grandfather arranged for a loan from some close Hungarian friends, the Doslops, and set off on his own. We never knew how much he paid for the land and the farmhouse—he wouldn't say—but a larger neighboring farm with a similar house sold for $800 at around the same time. Grandma was terrified of borrowing any amount of money, and of the responsibilities of ownership, but

Grandpa told her he could not stay in the same place at the same job for the rest of his life; it would have been a kind of surrender. Anyway, he was tired of working for other people, subject to the whims of management or malevolent coworkers. He was tired of working indoors under horrible conditions. He didn't mind long hours or the hard work, but he couldn't see spending all that time and effort for an hourly wage that might disappear for reasons having nothing to do with his dedication or his skills.

Right away, Grandpa decided he would grow a little of everything, which was the way people farmed in Hungary. It was the only kind of farming he knew, and that was lucky, since it was also the only kind of farming he could have managed on that land. The landscape was harsh, the weather unpredictable. There was no real cash crop. The farm was too small. He didn't have the luxury of planting fifty acres of corn and fifty acres of wheat to absorb a few mistakes. His plan was to simply grow as much of as many different crops as he could, and sell whatever was in surplus.

The farm was entirely hand-run and handmade. There was almost no machinery, and no money for outside resources. Grandpa made all his own tools and baskets and did his own repairs. If he couldn't make something himself or fix it himself, he'd find a way to do without it. Winters were spent fixing and crafting. Summers were for the work and the details.

All year long, the farm stood as one of the most peaceful places on earth. There were no cars; there were no planes overhead. The only sounds were those we made ourselves. My grandfather knew every vine, every rock, every tree, and he could sense if the slightest piece was out of place. He tended that farm as if it were a delicate still life. His haystacks, though functional, were works of art, as important to him for their symbolic beauty and their link to the farms of his childhood as they were for their intrinsic value. Americans put their hay in barns, but eastern Europeans stacked it outside, and Grandpa built his up into perfectly rounded sculptures. To him, they were an emblem of pride.

Haying was an event all its own. My father and grandfather would cut the hay with a scythe, and we kids would follow with the hay rakes. We didn't have straight-handled rakes (our rakes were only as straight as the branches of our trees, from which they were made), and we struggled behind, in the heat of summer, the dust from the hay sticking to our sweat and our clothes. I loved working on the farm, but haying was an awful job, and we tried to hide whenever it came around on the calendar. My father always knew where to find me. After we were through raking, he'd pitchfork the hay up onto the wagon, and Grandpa would take it back and fashion his perfect haystacks, which wound up looking like tall soft-serve ice cream cones. When we needed hay, we had to draw it from the back, so as not to upset the symmetry from the front.

My grandfather was still selling his fruits and vegetables from the back of a horse-drawn wagon up until I was about ten or so. Harry the horse, or any of his predecessors, was probably the biggest single investment on the farm: The horse pulled double-duty, drawing the plow through the fields and the wagon through the streets of Peekskill. Grandpa would ride behind Harry on his perfectly maintained wagon, which was repainted every season with whatever color paint we had in surplus. He would sell door-to-door until there was nothing left to sell, then head home to work the farm and load up his wares for the next morning, when he would leave before sunup. In my time, one or two grandchildren always rode with him, as helpers, and the job was handed down among us cousins each summer, from the oldest to the youngest. It never reached me. My cousins Freddy and Kerry were the last ones on the job, and they used to come back and tell the younger kids how Harry the horse knew exactly where to stop along the route. He even knew enough to stop across the street from a local bar, so that Grandpa could drink a couple of beers in the middle of the afternoon before heading home.

Every other night, after dinner, we gathered around a huge galvanized tub under a beautiful apple tree in front of my grandparents' porch and washed all the fruits and vegetables, then loaded them into baskets and onto the wagon for the next morning's trip into town.

Grandpa put all of us to work, when we were old enough; by the time I was ready, there were about a dozen cousins on our little assembly line, and we didn't quit until every last basket was full.

Grandpa was still heading downtown with his horse and wagon in the 1950s, long after cars had become the major method of transportation and long after he should have quit. It was an enduring sight: Janos Pataki, worn and stubborn, smoking his pipe packed with tobacco he had grown and cured himself, driving a wagon piled high with a fantastically colorful array of fresh fruits and vegetables. He was about seventy years old, and determined to beat back the modern world, but in the sound of the wagon's metal rims meeting the paved Bear Mountain Parkway he gave himself away. On the dirt paths of the farm, the wheels always made a gentle crunching sound as they rolled over the hard earth and small stones, but as soon as he pulled off the property it was a race against time; the rims hit the asphalt like the wrong shoes for a long hike, and the sound he left behind—Harry, clip-clopping on the double yellow lines of a four-lane highway—was out of place, slightly off. All around were haste and commerce and bustling activity, and Grandpa went about his business as if time had stood still.

The running argument in our family was that Grandpa was going to get killed making his rounds. There was too much traffic for a horse. For a long time, hardly anyone had used the Bear Mountain Parkway except us kids, for baseball. We'd set up our diamond right in the middle of the highway, and we could usually get in an inning or two without having to move for a passing car. But after a while the surrounding areas grew, the road became more popular with drivers, and we had to take our game elsewhere.

Grandpa, though, wasn't about to change his routine. Harry didn't know about stoplights or traffic rules; all he knew was home, and when he came near home he would just take off, sometimes at full gallop, straight across the parkway if that was what was in his way. Once, the horse caught his leg outside the stay, right at the corner of Broad and Main, one of the busiest intersections in Peekskill, and traffic was snarled for over an hour until my father could get off from his job at the post office a couple of blocks away and coax Harry's leg back over the stay. The resulting traffic jam was the end of the line for Grandpa's delivery route. He retired the wagon, put Harry out to pasture, and opened shop on the porch of the house; for the next thirty years people came from miles around to buy our fruits and vegetables.

There was still plenty of work for the horse. One of Harry's main jobs was to pull the plow through the fields, and I still cherish the rare opportunity to till a field with a horse and plow. Harry did this dependably until one afternoon when he ran into a beehive. He took off at full gallop, while my father ran behind, holding on to the back of the plow, like Ben-Hur without the chariot. Before Harry tired himself out, he had taken my father through three fields.

My father and grandfather could never agree on the economics of the farm. In season, the Pataki stand was usually sold out by midafternoon, right down to the tables. This was due, in part, to the high demand for the high-quality produce we put out for our customers, but it also had to do with the low yield on our small farm, which in turn had mostly to do with this constant debate. The farm was Grandpa's, so the last word was his, but he liked to think he was open to my father's ideas—or, at least, he liked my father to think so. Dad had a day job as a mailman, but he also put in a full day of work with my grandfather, and this sometimes led to a clash in philosophy. The aesthetics, to Grandpa, were all-important, while my father tended toward the practical. Dad was an American, and his impulse was to maximize productivity. Grandpa was European, and he would grow just enough that he could tend each plant individually. He staked and tied every single tomato plant—and we had 300 or 400 of them, which added up to a lot of stakes and ties. My father would plant 2,000 tomato plants and not stake or tie a single one, so he'd suffer a lot more loss, but he'd still wind up with a lot more tomatoes than my grandfather. His thinking was he'd get more out of 2,000 plants, losing half his crop, than Grandpa would get from 300 or 400, losing only 10 percent or so.

But Grandpa was a perfectionist, and the two of them battled over their philosophies for years, until simple pragmatism won out. We couldn't plant enough produce to keep up with our customers, once we shifted from the horse and wagon to the farm stand. We could have sold ten times what we had—raspberries, strawberries, peaches . . . everything sold out. Grandpa's emphasis on quality was highly appreciated by his customers. My cousin Freddy suggested that we adopt a kind of lottery system to meet the demand, but we ended up rationing what we had and trying to keep our good customers happy and coming back for more. If a man asked for a dozen ears of corn, we sold him six; if he complained, we told him to be grateful for the six, because he wasn't likely to get any more tomorrow.

Grandma handled the stand, and she was as hard on her grandchildren as she was on her customers. Our pay, after a day in the fields or loading baskets, was a homemade shortcake after dinner: strawberry, raspberry, or (my favorite) peach. We were happy to have it. She never let us kids near the money. For a long time, she wouldn't even let us near the raspberries. According to Grandma, that was a job for the grown-ups, because the slightest pressure might bruise the fruit. We could pick apples and peaches and corn; we could even pick strawberries, because you don't actually touch a strawberry. (You pinch the stem with your fingernails.)

But Grandma had it in her head that raspberry picking was a rite of passage to which we would never ascend. When I came home from Yale—a college boy!—she still fretted about whether I could handle the job. She thought my cousin Bobby's hands were too big; she thought he would squash her sensitive berries. One summer, after we had both started college, we finally managed to persuade her to let us help pick the raspberries. We'll be responsible, we promised. We'll do a good job. It was a point of pride to my cousin and me, but more than that it was a fantastic chance to tweak Grandma's expectations of our limited abilities, a practical joke waiting to happen.

Eventually, Grandma relented, so Bobby and I went out to pick some raspberries. As it happened, we had the best berries that year— big, colorful, and juicy. For the most part, we did do a good job, but we took a few of the berries from a few of the baskets and crushed them with our hands. Then we set the mashed berries back on top and let the juice run down, so that the baskets were stained and the good berries were all sticky.

"Grandma," Bobby said, presenting her with a sample of our effort, his voice full of mischief, "look at the wonderful raspberries we picked."

Grandma didn't see too well (a trait I inherited, along with her blind optimism and her willingness to give people the benefit of the doubt), and she took one look at the raspberries and joined in our enthusiasm. Then she took a closer look and nearly choked. "My raspberries!" she screamed. "You've ruined my raspberries! I knew I should never let you pick the berries!" It took the rest of the afternoon to convince her that it was a joke.

The story has stayed with me for the way it illustrates the exacting nature of the Pataki farm, and the underlying ethic. My grandmother's concern for her precious berries flowed directly from my grandfather. After all, it was his high standard she was trying to uphold. It was Grandpa who insisted that we place the best strawberries or raspberries or apples on the *bottom* of our baskets, when every other farmer put the best fruit on top. To Grandpa, it was the difference between packaging and value, flash and substance. His thinking was that you should deliver more than people expect, so that they come away pleasantly surprised instead of disappointed.

He was that way about everything. He would never let us sell a peach or an apple that had fallen off a tree. This was an absolute rule. We'd pick an apple up from the ground, and it would be absolutely perfect because the grass underneath was so soft, but he wouldn't hear of selling it. If it's not from the tree, he used to say, it's not from the tree. We'd either eat it ourselves or use it to make cider or applesauce. As I recall, we made an awful lot of sauce.

Grandpa's values were ennobling, but they were not without a price. Some years they were particularly devastating. We grew a lot of McIntosh apples, and McIntoshes have a tendency to fall early. A lot of farmers treated them with hormones, to help them stay on the trees in a cold snap or a brisk wind, but we wouldn't do that. With the exception of a rare application of pesticides to the fruit trees and a spraying of the tomatoes, Grandpa's farm was all natural. Everything was organic, long before anyone used that term. We had a pile of horse manure, and a pile of cow manure. Cow manure was great, because you could use it right away; horse manure you had to leave for a few years, but this was okay with us kids because it made a fine worm pile. We also saved ashes from the wood-burning stove in my grandparents' house and placed them at the bottom of the grapevines; wood ash was a fine source of potash, which was good for the plants. My grandfather couldn't afford commercial fertilizer, even if he hadn't been opposed to it, so we'd have beautiful trees with gorgeous McIntoshes, and we'd get a wind one night and half the apples would fall to the ground. The only way to salvage our investment was to make cider, and McIntoshes make terrible cider.

The truth always found us on the farm. We'd have a great peach crop, and then we'd get a hailstorm. We'd cut a field of hay, by hand, only to have the skies open up without warning, ruining the whole day's work. On our farm, as on any other, we could never rely on a thing until it actually happened. This has become a maxim that informs my public life. I am constantly trying to improve on my campaign promises, or I promise less than I know I can deliver. In my first year as governor, I was committed to a balanced budget, but I was actually determined to deliver a surplus. And we did. I was tougher on crime than I said I was going to be. My administration reduced taxes beyond what had been anticipated. As a matter of fact, in 1996 and again in 1997, our tax cuts outpaced cuts in the other forty-nine states combined, but we didn't promise that, and we didn't take out ads trumpeting that; we wanted people to come to it on their own, because in politics—as in life, as in farming—it is sometimes sensible to count on less and be pleasantly surprised with more. And, by extension, it is foolish to count on anything until you have it in hand.

Our entire culture, it seems, has been built more and more on imagery, from government on down. It's all glitz and show. It's putting the big berries on top of the basket and hoping people won't have time to get to the bottom, or that they won't remember the contrast by the time they do. This is very different from what I was taught. In politics, I find it extremely difficult to stand up and crow about one accomplishment or another, because I want people to discover for themselves that what is happening is better than what they expected. I firmly believe that what matters is not who gets credit for implementing change, but the change itself.

I realize that such convictions cast me as something of an anomaly—perhaps even a naive bumpkin. This is simply not the way things are done in politics, certainly not if you want to get yourself reelected. But a farmer who crows about a crop before it's picked is being foolish. A farmer must take the long view. A farmer–turned–lawyer–turned–elected official should do the same. It's not what you say, it's what you do. Constituents remember campaign promises and false hopes, just as customers remember being suckered at a farm stand. If what you want is long-term respect, you've got to earn it with hard work, and by degrees. When I decided to run for governor, it was only after a succession of low-key roles in state government, during which people came to know that I meant what I said and that I would do my best to come through. I suppose there were glitzier candidates on the scene, and higher-profile candidates, and better-financed candidates, but there were pieces missing in their foundations. With me, it was all about the foundation.

Mario Cuomo won national attention and respect with his powerful speeches—but as it turned out, with him, all the big berries were on the top of the basket. Any respect I may earn will come not from a speech but from a record, a foundation, built from the bottom up. I couldn't sleep at night if all I had to go on was a new coat of paint or a shallow pledge, and I got that way from my father, and he got it from his father. We all had it, on the farm: work, not glitz; solutions, not blame; results, not talk. It's what had us putting the big berries in the bottom of the basket. It's what had us planting tomatoes in April, hoping that one year they would make it through. It's what had us looking ahead, never looking back and never counting ourselves out.

3

On the River

MY MOTHER'S PARENTS OFFERED A COUNTERBALANCE, AND a counterpoint, to the Pataki ethic. They were both terrific characters.

My maternal grandfather, Matteo Lagana, was born in Pelaro, just outside Reggio di Calabria, Italy, in what was also an incredibly poor village. For some reason, Calabrians were known as unusually headstrong—*testa dura,* or to the Calabrians themselves, *capatesto.* This was a taunt heard frequently in my grandfather's region, and it was tossed good-naturedly around our house as well. And yet when I went back to visit my grandfather's childhood home, I found the locals friendly and no more thickheaded than the rest of us.

There were seven in Grandpa's family, living in a cramped two-room house on a dirt street above the village. I keep a charming painting of the Calabria house in my office; in the artist's eye, there was something romantic about the time and place, but in truth it was harsh and unrelenting.

My grandfather came to America in October 1908, at the age of twelve. He had only ten dollars in his pocket, so between them my two grandfathers' stake in America was about twenty-one dollars. Despite his young age, my Italian grandfather had left home on his own impulse—his leaving had nothing to do with any larger family plan—and he wound up staying with a cousin and working as a stable hand on a horse farm in Mount Kisco, in Westchester County. In 1908, in Calabria and other southern regions of Italy, nonagricultural jobs were low-paying and hard to find. The government had started to tax essential items such as bread, making it extremely difficult for the peasant classes to get by. In many ways, my grandfather had no choice but to look elsewhere for opportunity, and the call of plentiful jobs and decent wages at American mines and factories was too rich to ignore. As I write this now, I find it hard to look away from the symmetry that sometimes exists between generations; to be sure, the runaway taxes that drove my grandfather from his homeland would later drive his grandson to a career in government.

From Mount Kisco, he got a job as a domestic aide to an upper-class family in Manhattan, and that's where he met my grandmother, Agnes Casey Lynch, who was working for the same family as a member of the household staff. My grandmother was born to Owen and Agnes Lynch in Ireland, just outside Black Rock in County Louth—another very rural, very poor community. She was one of nine children, and once again the way to a better life was clearly in America, as it was for so many Irish families. The oldest child, Mary, came over, married a Kelly in Brooklyn, and worked to send for the next in line. The second child, May, arrived in New York, and then the third, who, sadly, contracted tuberculosis and died soon after; this meant that the first two had to dip into their scant savings to pay for the doctor and the funeral, and then start saving again to bring the next sibling over.

The fourth child in the Lynch clan was one of my grandmother's older sisters, Bridgit, and the family story is that she was especially attached to her father. Her crossing to America had been discussed, and arranged, but Bridgit couldn't bring herself to leave. As the whole family was preparing to see her off, she clung to my great-grandfather Owen's legs and refused to go.

"I can't leave you," she cried. "I love you! I won't go!"

My grandmother, who was sixth or seventh in line, stepped up and said to her sister, "I know how close you are to Dad. I'll go in your place." And she did.

My grandmother traveled with her sister's papers, and therefore her sister's name, and as it turned out she was the last sibling to make the trip. At first there wasn't enough money to bring the next sibling over, and soon the others were settled into new lives and relationships, and as the years went by the notion of coming to America probably appeared less attainable—or maybe it seemed to matter less. The frustrating footnote to my grandmother's story was that we could never locate her immigration papers through the Ellis Island Foundation, and the reason, of course, was that she had entered the country under her sister's name.

This was never more than a bother to our family over the years, and yet Grandma's story actually made headlines on the eve of the 1996 Republican National Convention in San Diego, when it was widely reported that I was the grandson of an illegal immigrant. The press immediately wanted to know my position on this important issue. To my thinking, someone born in America is an American. How can we treat a child born in New York or Chicago (or Peekskill) as a foreigner simply because the parents' papers are not in order? After all, what is an American? We are linked by our common values and language, our ideal of freedom, respect for democracy, our belief in America, and our commitment to what it stands for. We are joined by the very fact of our being here. My grandmother was proud to be an American, and her children were proud to be Americans; this grandchild is proud to be an American too.

Perhaps I'm overly patriotic, or maybe too trusting, but I believe people from around the world are drawn to America by the light of freedom. They come here because they want to be a part of the dream, because they see a chance through education and work to build a better future. The federal government has an obligation to uphold and enforce the immigration laws of this country to ensure that those who come to America seeking freedom and opportunity do so legally. These laws, however, must be squarely and solely aimed at fulfilling that purpose. They must never infringe on the right of individuals to pursue for themselves and their children the principles of freedom and liberty on which America was founded.

It didn't matter to me or my mother how my grandmother came to America—only that she came. And it mattered that, once here, she wanted to make the best of it, so she looked for what work she could find. After a time, she hired on as a maid for the same family for whom my grandfather was working as a butler, and there they met and fell in love. I guess you could call it an office romance; that's the way it filtered down to us. Whatever it was, they were a good fit. They were both blessed with a fiery spirit, a longing for a more independent life, and a refreshing tolerance for each other.

They moved from one wealthy family to the next, as butler and maid, and it seemed to Grandma that they had a good thing going. She didn't want much—only to be working, and healthy, in America with her young husband. One summer, with the wealthy family of the moment vacationing in Europe, my grandparents were left as caretakers of a palatial summer home in the country. They had the whole estate to themselves, and there was nothing for Grandpa to do but run up the American flag in the morning and take it down at night. Grandma remembered it as an idyllic summer, and she looked forward to many more like it; to her, there were a great many benefits to a life in the employ of the idle rich. But to Grandpa that summer was a nagging reminder that his own life would never truly begin until he stopped working for someone else—especially when there was no work to be done.

When the boss and his family returned from Europe, Grandpa proudly offered his resignation. Grandma couldn't believe it. "What in God's name are you doing?" she asked. "This is a great job. This is a great place to live. We can raise a family, working for these good people."

"I didn't come to America to be someone else's servant," he announced. "That I could have done in Italy."

And so they moved on, from one moneymaking scheme to the next—not all of them within the boundaries of the law. They ran a shoeshine stand and later a bar, and for a number of years during Prohibition Grandpa set up a small distillery in the tub. One of my mother's first jobs, when she was six or seven years old, was to put Gordon's Gin labels on the bottles my grandparents sold; my Aunt Aggie, Mom's older sister, made the neighborhood deliveries. My mother's teachers were amazed, when she got to high school, that she already knew how to use a hydrometer. They never knew why. It was never more than a nickel-and-dime family effort, and yet it was a way to get by, and I consider it now in context. Right or wrong, the making, selling, and drinking of alcoholic beverages remained common practice in polite (and not-so-polite) society throughout Prohibition; indeed, many famous fortunes were built from the slow drip of a home distillery.

I learned all of this from my grandmother in a strange way. One summer, when I was back at home after my freshman year at Yale, I sat down with her to catch up. Out of nowhere, she broke into the Harvard fight song. "Grandma," I asked, in shock, "how did you learn the Harvard fight song?"

It was a long story. In the early days, before they quit their jobs as domestics, my grandparents made booze for an exclusive clientele: The family they worked for had a son at Harvard, and he enlisted my grandparents to help supply his college pals. It was, according to my grandmother, a neat operation: The son would call home to New York City and say he had forgotten his overcoat, or his books, and ask to have Matt the butler bring them up. Then my enterprising grandparents would head out with the overcoat and books and a suitcase full of gin. Once they'd made the trip, they'd spend the weekend with the Harvard boys, drinking up the atmosphere and a good deal of the profits. In this way, my illiterate grandparents became the first in our family to receive an Ivy League education.

It was into this sort of free-spirited ethic that my mother was born, and she spent most of her childhood in the immigrant tenements of Manhattan, near the Third Avenue El, with a shared bathroom down the hall and the entire city as her backyard. The tenements housed virtually every new immigrant group coming to New York—Greek, Jewish, Polish, Irish, Italian. The building was its own melting pot: My mother's godfather was a Russian Jew named Morris Horowitz. At my mother's christening, the story goes, the priest remarked that Horowitz didn't exactly sound like a Catholic name, to which the new godfather replied, "From now on, just call me Murphy." And from that day until his death fifty years later, Morris Horowitz was always called Murphy.

In New York City, my mother was free to roam, and to dream. It was a world away from my father's childhood—and yet somehow those worlds came together in Peekskill, in a diner run by my aunt's family, where my father worked as a dishwasher and my mother as a waitress. Another office romance. They, too, were a fine match—fond of hard work, and family, and each other. They were so fond of their families, in fact, they encouraged my maternal grandparents to move to Peekskill, so that they could be nearby, and by the time I was born Grandpa Matt and Grandma Aggie were living in a house at the back of the Pataki spread, on abutting farmland my grandfather had purchased simply to be close to his daughter and her family. He had no intention of farming that land, but there was a nice enough house on it, and it was as good a place to live as any.

Even after my parents had met and married, my mother's parents still scrambled to make a living. Grandpa always seemed to be straining for the next big thing. He seemed to need to struggle, to stretch. It was what kept him alive. My Italian grandfather owned half the establishments in Peekskill, at one time or another, but that was precisely the problem: He owned them at one time or another, one at a time, so he was never quite a man of means. The idea, presumably, was to trade up, but sometimes he just traded one holding for another. At one time or another, he owned an antiques store, a restaurant, the old Dolan Hotel, a few commercial buildings, a Chinese hand laundry . . . all kinds of places. If the building housed a going concern, he did what he could to run it. He'd put everything he had into a broken-down operation, fix it up, and sell it—sometimes for a small profit, sometimes not. It used to drive my poor grandmother mad, since she was charged with most of the fixing up.

Although he lacked any formal education beyond third grade, Grandpa Matt thought himself something of an architect—and an engineer, and a lawyer, whatever. He'd have a real architect draw up plans for a renovation and then go out and do it his way. He was, after all, Calabrian. He put in septic tanks upside down, doors hinged the wrong way, whatever seemed like a good idea at the time. He couldn't read or write English. He couldn't read or write Italian. He couldn't read or write anything. (I once saw him behind an upside-down newspaper, pretending to read it.) But he usually had a deal cooking, and he usually came out whole. He was extremely proud to be an American, and he would speak only English, even though he was almost impossible to understand. Nevertheless, I was very proud of the fact that he tried so hard. Curiously, three American presidents had vetoed literacy as a requirement for immigration into this country; if any one of them had seen things another way, my Italian grandfather could not have entered the United States.

When I was a kid, he bought a piece of land down by the Hudson River, on King's Ferry Road in Verplanck, just south of Peekskill, which he turned into a workingman's boat club. That he was drawn to the river at all was telling. He had grown up on the straits of Messina, an incredibly beautiful area looking over to Mount Etna and the Sicilian mountains beyond. But he remembered the water as inaccessible, something he could enjoy only from a distance. It was the same on King's Ferry Road. The Hudson was also beautiful from a distance, and relatively inaccessible; the property had plenty of riverfront, but the water was so filthy no one wanted to go near it. My aunt used to call the place the Pigeon S--- Yacht Club, for the way Grandpa's cherished birds decorated the landscape. He always kept pigeons, atop every building he had access to, and they always made a mess; considering the condition of the river itself, the bird droppings were an oddly appropriate touch.

The irony of operating a not-quite-full-service marina on the Hudson River was lost on my grandfather. The water was too dirty to swim in, and we were too poor to own a boat, but Grandpa could work a pile driver and nail boards together to make a dock, so he figured a boat club was a good idea. It wasn't really. Most of the working-class people in town were in no position to own a boat, and most of them had trouble with the concept of leisure time, so a boat club was hard to sell at first—especially to my grandmother, who couldn't see the logic of it. But Grandpa kept at it. He targeted the blue-collar crowd with small boats and dinghies and gave them his best pitch. The fishing was lousy, he admitted, but the crabbing was okay, and the weather wasn't too bad, and there was a decent bar on the other side of the river, and if you timed it right you could cross the river, down a couple of beers, snare a couple of crabs, and cross back to dry land before low tide turned Grandpa's corner of the Hudson to muck. His property jutted out into a little inlet called Green's Cove, and the water level there was often low, even at high tide. Still, he persuaded enough of his Italian and Irish friends to give the King's Ferry Boat Club a try that he was able to keep the marina going. He eventually added a bar and a restaurant and a few apartments; it wasn't exactly a class operation, but it was an operation.

By the time I was ten or twelve, my grandparents had moved off the mosquito-infested swamp adjacent to the Pataki farm—a spot that my aunt, who was never very generous in her assessment of a situation, had dubbed "Hellhole Hollow"—and set up housekeeping at the boat club. It sounded glamorous to be living on the water, but that was deceiving. The air smelled of sewage, dead fish, and rotten eggs; pigeon droppings were everywhere; and there was a list of repairs that sometimes seemed to run the length of the river itself.

What little money the place generated came in drips. Those who couldn't afford Grandpa's docking fee were encouraged to work it off in trade, or to barter. He never turned away a "good customer," but I never understood his definition of the term. I couldn't imagine how he took a paycheck out of that place. The King's Ferry "members" couldn't imagine it either; they just didn't understand how my grandfather tracked their payments, and some of them made a game out of trying to beat his system, whatever it was. His bellowing could be heard across what there was of the water whenever someone was in arrears: "You haven't paid! You owe me money!" Except that in his thick Italian accent, the words didn't sound quite like this.

Yet, somehow, my grandfather knew. He obviously couldn't keep any written records, and he accepted only cash, but people would skulk around like deadbeats if they were late with their payments. It took a friend of my father's from the post office to crack Grandpa's system. One day, Dad's friend, who hadn't paid the fee, was at the dock. He was standing with another man who *had* paid, and my grandfather started ranting at the guy who had paid up: "You owe me money! I'll take your boat and use it for firewood!"

Dad's friend broke out laughing. He had finally figured it out. Grandpa used colored thumbtacks to track his rent roll. If you paid, you got a thumbtack of one color tacked into the dock by your boat; if you didn't, you got another color. It was simple enough. Dad's friend just switched tacks and set my grandfather's accounting system back a couple of months—and the other man's blood boiled.

Grandpa's boat club was a constant reminder of the scandalous condition of the Hudson River, which was a great waterway only in memory. At high tide in Green's Cove, the river rose to only about six or eight feet, so there was hardly enough draw for some of the bigger fishing boats—but then, you wouldn't want to eat the fish you caught there anyway. At low tide, there was maybe a couple of inches of water, and all around you could see bottles and rusted gas tanks and all kinds of debris sunk into the river bottom. It was filthy. We were afraid to dip our toes into the water. I learned to swim in Peekskill's municipal pool, and every time I set off on the 2½-mile walk from our farm to the pool I got to thinking about the river. It was a shame, I realized even then, to have the mighty Hudson outside my grandfather's back door and to be unable to enjoy it.

That was the paradox of life on the river. Communities like Peekskill had been born on the strength of the Hudson, and yet those communities very nearly killed it. In the beginning, the river was

Peekskill's front porch—the gateway to wide-open spaces—but it quickly became the back porch, the repository for sewers, waste, and garbage. We were all guilty. I remember working at the Fleischmann's factory during vacations, and if someone turned the wrong valve you could actually see an overflow of brown or green sludge pour into the river below. Everyone just assumed that industrial waste would float downstream and become someone else's problem, but the river paid for our neglect—and so did we.

In my public life, I've made it a priority to restore the river to its "front porch" status and to make protection of our environment—clean air, clean water, open spaces—one of the government's main concerns. We've done a lot to revive the river, to expand parklands, to increase public access. When I was in the legislature, I was a cosponsor of the Hudson River Estuary Management Act, which directs state and local officials to consider the river as a whole, to consider how our upland and wetland areas interrelate with our urban stretches, and since then enormous progress has been made in cleaning up the riverbed and the surrounding valley. New York State has created the Hudson River Greenway to provide and maintain trails reaching from Manhattan to the Adirondacks, so that people can enjoy and help to preserve the habitat. It has actively bought up open spaces and up-graded sewage treatment plants throughout the state, including along the Hudson. And in 1997, for the first time in a hundred years, a bald eagle was born in the Hudson Valley.

I can't think of a better investment in our shared future—or a more fulfilling legacy for my time in office. I remember writing to the conservation commissioners in almost every state when I was a kid, hoping to get back brochures in the return mail. I couldn't type, but I hunted and pecked until I produced a letter asking for maps, brochures, or pictures of state parks and open spaces. Every return package was an adventure. I've always loved maps and local histories, and these state brochures were small treasures. I'd tape them to the wall, next to my baseball cards, and lose myself in the wonders of the great outdoors.

Of course, I don't claim credit for the Hudson's rehabilitation, but

I am proud to have played a role. The effort started before me, in the 1960s, with Nelson Rockefeller's Clean Water Bond Act, which marked the first time a state had committed significant funds to help local governments improve waterways. And my administration is building on that beginning, committing billions to clean up the Hudson and Long Island Sound, for clean air projects, and to preserve important open spaces. I look on it as analogous to a blue chip company's investing in itself and buying back its own stock, and on my watch the state has bought back some key parcels in the Adirondacks and a mile or so of shoreline along Lake George. We bought a major wildlife sanctuary out in Montauk, at the easternmost tip of Long Island, helping to make more than 50 percent of that area owned, protected, or preserved by the state. We also purchased a half mile of pristine Lake Erie beachfront, just a mile or so south of Buffalo, creating the first new state park in western New York in more than fifty years.

And we're not stopping there. As of this writing, we've reached agreement to buy a dramatic tract in the heart of the Hudson Valley known as Sterling Forest, which marks the single largest addition to our state park system in the past hundred years and will create an unparalleled, unbroken wilderness reaching down into northern New Jersey. We've also agreed to purchase a part of the 51,000 Adirondack acres owned by the Whitney estate, which will add yet another strand to the necklace of parkland in that region.

As a teenager, I walked the ridges and peaks of Bull Hill, with its magnificent views of the Hudson Highlands and Valley. It's wonderful to know that someday my grandchildren will be able to take those same hikes and see the same views as I did. And the key to the buyback program is just that: The state *buys* the land. We don't pass a regulation telling the people who own this land, "Tough luck—you can't do anything with it." We don't condemn the land or find some other way to claim it for the state. There are those who believe in big government, who would strong-arm private landowners and gain effective government control without paying a dime or by foreclosing on below-market deals; but we try to give fair value. Obviously, we encourage people to donate tracts of land, which happens from time to time, but we have a sound (and fair) strategy of purchasing land in place.

Some of the state's biggest environmental initiatives, ironically enough, have been driven by technology. We're converting the entire fleet of New York City–area Metropolitan Transit Authority buses to low-emission vehicles. We've pushed the EZ-Pass program, allowing bridge and highway tolls to be collected electronically; by now, this is the preferred method of payment, and traffic has been improved. When you think back, the ability to make a right turn after stopping at a red light grew out of the gasoline crisis in the middle 1970s; instead of sitting there idling, you could make a turn and save gas. We're seeing some of the same benefits by dramatically reducing the wait at our toll plazas. We're even getting cars off the streets, with the MetroCard program that has now eliminated the two-fare zone—for people who had to take a bus to the subway—from the daily commute of thousands of New Yorkers. Our subways and buses are attracting more riders, at these lower fares; we're cutting down on traffic and pollution; and people are saving time and hundreds of dollars each year—so it's been a tremendous success all around.

Underneath each and every environmental effort is a scene from my childhood, an incentive to ensure that future generations have it better than we did as kids. We need to leave the land richer and cleaner for our having been here, and this goes for our waterways as well. As a boy, I was down by the river all the time during the summer, and yet we might as well have been docking boats alongside a painting of a river for all the time we got to spend on the water. It would have been funny if it weren't so sad. I'd worked on and around boats all my life, but I don't think I actually took a boat out for a ride more than two or three times until I graduated from high school. By then, we'd picked up an old rowboat and outfitted it with a two-horsepower motor, and we puttered around on summer nights. The Navy used to keep a ghost fleet of World War Two liberty ships—about a hundred of them—moored over in Tompkins Cove, awaiting the next international crisis, and we'd maneuver our little boat around those great vessels all night long. It was great fun, and an uncommon view. It wasn't as if we were tourists, sitting up on the bridge of a cabin cruiser, contemplating naval history. From our lowly perspective, we really developed a feel for the water, and for the majesty of the fleet. The Hudson would slosh over the sides of our boat, and I'd look up at the hulls of those great ships and marvel at the rest of the world.

But we would never go into the water unless we had to, or unless we fell in. Now this has changed.

While I learned much about the environment from being outside with my Grandpa, Grandma taught me much about life, and tolerance. She had a truly wonderful sense of humor and indomitable vigor. She was always laughing and spinning tales in her thick Irish brogue. Before they moved down to the river, I used to trek down the dirt road that connected our properties to have tea and toast with my grandmother. This became our special time together. I was old enough to go unannounced, and often did, but Grandma was always ready for me. She baked her own bread and cut her toast about an inch and a half thick, and I can remember biting into those big pieces and wiping the slather of butter or jam dripping down my chin and thinking this was the finest treat in all the world. And the tea! It all seemed so very dignified, so refined, to an eight-year-old boy, to be sipping tea and talking. That was the best part—to sit back and listen to Grandma's stories of how it was when she was a girl—because in her tales I found a kind of awakening. I grew up knowing I was Irish as well as Italian and Hungarian. Grandma made sure of that, and her stories became a part of me.

"Grandma," I once asked her around St. Patrick's Day, "did you always have corned beef and cabbage when you were in Ireland?"

"No, Georgie," she said. "I never had beef in me life. The British stole every bit. We had cabbage. We had potatoes. If we were lucky we had pork."

Grandma didn't care much for life under the hard rule of the British. She grew up in County Louth, which is on the border separating the Catholic south from the Protestant north. One story was emblematic. When she was a little girl, at the back end of eight brothers and sisters, she heard a knock at the door. It was late at night, and the small house thundered with the intrusion. Her father was off working, and her mother was looking after the children, and Grandma remembered peering out from her room to understand the commotion. There were often strange threatening noises in the middle of the night, and it was a comfort to Grandma to find out what they were. On this night, though, there was only confusion, because there at the front door she saw two British soldiers and her mother—a strong, independent woman who had never shrunk from a confrontation—on her knees, crying, begging. It was, my grandmother recalled, the most frightening moment of her young life, to see her proud mother reduced to such helplessness, such fear.

Apparently, some young kids had kicked over the tombstones in a nearby Protestant cemetery and the soldiers had come for one of my grandmother's brothers. They hadn't come to ask questions; they had come for *him*, to take him away. My great-grandmother pleaded with the soldiers and somehow managed to convince them that her son was not involved, and the matter was later dropped, but what stayed with my grandmother and what she passed on to me was the arbitrariness of it all. There would be no trial, no justice, no hearing by your peers. This was, to her family, the most agonizing frustration. Her brother had not been seen near the cemetery that night, but he was known to run around with a republican (even then) crowd, those who were willing to fight for Ireland's freedom; and the government had absolute power to take a kid, a teenager, away from his parents and deport him halfway around the world, never to be seen again.

I thought of that night again in 1996, when I signed the Irish Starvation Law, requiring New York public schools to teach students about the discrimination against the Catholics in Ireland, and to consider the nineteenth-century potato famine alongside other violations of human rights, from slavery to the Holocaust. I think of that night still. Indeed, the story of the tombstones and the British soldiers—or, more accurately, the lesson of that story—is with me all the time, because it personalizes for me what most of us take for granted. To be truly free a nation must be built on a limited government acting as a

benevolent force—helping people, protecting them from nongovern-
mental tyranny and exploitation—as opposed to a government that
has the power to take away our liberties.

What kind of life would it be if we lived in fear of the government,
as my grandmother lived in Ireland? A limited government as envi-
sioned by the Founding Fathers must be the ideal, but even in America
it is not always the reality. I am not alone in believing that too many of
our local, state, and federal government officials have lost touch with
the people they were meant to serve. No, it's not the way it was for my
grandmother; government is not pounding on people's doors late at
night, meting out arbitrary punishment. But we must remain ever
vigilant, because the line between a benevolent government and an
oppressive one is not always clear. Here in the United States, our
founders were extraordinarily brilliant in setting up the system of
checks and balances within our Constitution. It keeps us honest. We
want to be sure that their vision remains the reality.

I think about my maternal grandparents, about how incredibly
brave my grandfather was to come to this country as a twelve-year-old
boy, without knowing the language or the customs; about my grandmother, coming as she did without notice, without knowing if she
would ever see her family, her friends, or her village again. It took
tremendous courage to do what they did, to build a life out of no life at
all, and they did it because they saw in America not just freedom but
opportunity, because they recognized a way out of the limits and oppression of their childhood and into the light of hope and plenty.

These were the lessons my grandparents, full of the promise of
America, passed down to me by the way they lived their lives, by
what they chose to share.

4

The Campaign

M Y DECISION TO RUN FOR GOVERNOR HAD EVERYTHING TO
do with the paths my grandparents had chosen; in a sense, I
had no choice but to run. The New York of my youth, a special place
which attracted people from across the country and around the world,
was being lost. The right we had as New Yorkers and Americans to believe that tomorrow would be better, if not for ourselves, certainly for
our children, was being lost to policies that were failing our future.

The 1994 campaign for governor of New York drew national attention and for good reason. I knew that for me to win as a Republican in
New York, with 2 million more registered Democrats than Republicans, our campaign had to be about ideas, about policies, a true debate
about the role of government in the future of our state. To me it was
simple—get across the ideas I believed in and knew were right for the
people, and I would win. It had to be about the fact that the race for
governor is not just a game of rhetoric or recrimination, but entails a
serious debate and critical choices affecting the future course of almost
18 million people.

And nowhere in America was the clash of different ideas or policies more evident than in New York State. Mario Cuomo was not just

the darling of the Democrats and the liberals (and much of the media); he had had twelve years to use New York as a testing ground for the strength or weakness of his liberal philosophy. With a legislature sympathetic to his big-government philosophy, there had been no effective check on his reign as the leading liberal executive in America.

And the reign had been a disaster! In Cuomo's New York, too many criminals could be convicted of a violent felony—not just charged, but tried and convicted—and not serve a day in jail. In the name of saving money, or a misguided sense of compassion, violent criminals could get out on early release or work release. And you didn't need a job to get out on work release. Repeat violent felons could be paroled.

And that was just criminals who were convicted. Absurd court decisions by Cuomo's liberal judges made it harder in New York than in any other state in America for the police to arrest, or for prosecutors to convict, those clearly guilty of violent crimes. And for twelve years, Mario Cuomo vetoed the death penalty bill sent him annually by the legislature.

Mario Cuomo had put in place one of the most generous of all welfare systems. It was a program that didn't go on just for months or years, but too often from generation to generation. Its benefit level was higher than almost any other state's, and of course there was no requirement that able-bodied participants engage in workfare in exchange for New York's beneficence. One in eleven residents in New York were on welfare, a completely unsustainable number. We had expansive government with expensive programs and unlimited budgets that grew at three times the rate of inflation every year of Cuomo's reign.

Such was Mario Cuomo's New York, with a "compassionate" welfare system, a criminal justice system that understood the "root" causes of crime, and an all-knowing government that kept growing voraciously to fill the need of a dependent people. And with what results? What consequences had flowed from twelve years of such liberal compassion? Exactly what I had expected. But not the rosy picture painted for years by a fawning national media elite.

New York's "understanding" criminal justice system had created streets unsafe even in midday, parks where parents were afraid to send their kids. Whole communities, even schools, ravaged by crime. And ironically it was just those low-income minority communities that were most ravaged by the criminals for whom the liberals had such understanding.

New York's caring welfare system had sapped incentives, penalized initiative, and created long-term dependency in a permanently poor population, an underclass that seemed to lack not just material things but spirit or belief in itself.

And New York's all-encompassing government? To feed its appetite New York's tax burden had been raised to the point where our people paid the highest taxes in America. Every fiscal gimmick was used, even "selling" Attica Prison from one state agency to another for $150 million in a desperate attempt to balance the budget and keep feeding the beast. As a consequence, New York was hit hard by the recession of the late 1980s; and even after the recession, between April 1989 and November 1994, while the rest of the nation was creating 6.7 million new jobs, New York State suffered almost 428,000 more lost jobs. First in taxation, last in jobs. Such was Mario Cuomo's New York—such was the New York I rejected, and that I knew we could change.

When you think about it, Mario Cuomo's life had not been that different from mine—he was a child of immigrants, informed by hard work and purpose—and yet he would reject logical conclusions, self-evident to most others, probably because they *were* self-evident and a "smart" person needed to be smarter than the rest and come to a different conclusion. He had to reject initiatives like longer sentences to reduce crime and workfare as a way to lower dependency. He had to reject the conventional wisdom in the relationship between raising taxes and losing jobs, because the conclusion was just too obvious.

The issues I campaigned on were the issues I'd grown up with. Jobs. Crime. Responsibility. Hope. Justice. I hated the way our welfare system had destroyed our work ethic; the way felons were returned to the streets blaming society for their transgressions instead of themselves; the way practical, fair-minded solutions were too often rejected in favor of political expedience or correctness. I hated the way dreams that were once rooted in promise and opportunity (my grandparents' dreams!) had now become the stuff of fantasy.

I jumped into the 1994 campaign with the unshakable belief that Mario Cuomo was a flawed leader. He may have been a skilled politician and orator, but that never translated into leadership. Obviously, he was a bright, capable person, but for all his pomp and eloquence he seemed always to see issues through a too-personal lens. His administration didn't appear to be about changing the state for the better as much as it was about lifting the public perception of Mario Cuomo. I had a chance to watch him in the legislature, and I wasn't impressed. Yes, Mario Cuomo could sometimes galvanize a room with his speeches, but his words were just poetry, when what New York needed was prose. He made the distinction himself, but he failed to see his own point. I studied Cuomo carefully all those years, before I tried to unseat him as governor. I wanted to see what all the fuss was about, what we Republicans were up against, but all I saw was condescension. I saw an unwillingness to listen to legitimate criticism, to recognize other points of view. I saw smoke and mirrors and Scotch tape. I listened to his "state of the state" addresses, and they didn't strike me as brilliant. They were fluff—poetry, not prose. They might sound wonderful on the evening news at home on TV, but they didn't create jobs in Buffalo or make the streets safer in Brooklyn.

There was no question in my mind, as early as 1990, that Mario Cuomo could be beaten, and in my private moments I looked at the field and felt that I was the one to oppose him. I hadn't been positioning myself for a run as governor; being a minority assemblyman from Peekskill didn't exactly identify me as a likely challenger. But timing and circumstance seemed to point in my direction, and I was motivated and pragmatic enough not to turn away. The more I looked at it, the more I wanted to run against Cuomo in 1990—I was convinced he was leading the state in the wrong direction and believed I had the ideas, the message, and the record that could beat him. Maybe it was planting tomatoes on April 1st, but I didn't think so.

Others apparently agreed with me. A group of assembly and senate Republicans asked me to run against him in January 1990. Even our new tough state Republican chairman, Pat Barrett, asked me to consider it.

I sat down with my own hastily convened group of advisers to figure what resources were available to us, and what ability the party had to raise money. Cuomo was vulnerable, I was certain, just as New Jersey senator Bill Bradley would prove vulnerable in 1992, in a narrow victory over a virtual unknown named Christie Todd Whitman. With the right message and messenger, all it would take was a well-run campaign, which in turn meant a well-financed campaign. So I went to Pat Barrett and made my interest clear. "I'll run," I said, "if the party can guarantee to raise $500,000 for the campaign."

Pat Barrett had done me the favor of naming me chairman of the Republican Platform Committee, an opportunity which gave me the chance to move all across the state and talk with the media. "George," Barrett said, "I can't guarantee you a specific amount. We'll do our best, but there are no guarantees." To his credit, Pat told the truth. No false promises, unlike what the Republican nominee, Andy O'Rourke, had been told in 1986.

I don't think I'd raised more than $50,000 for a campaign in my life, and with my limited social and business contacts I doubted very seriously that I could do much better this time out. Even $500,000 was an absurdly small, bare-bones figure (as it turned out, the 1994 campaign cost more than $15 million), but if the state chairman couldn't promise even that, we were doomed from the start. I could be the best candidate, running with the best ideas, but with no resources I would never unseat a name-brand incumbent like Mario Cuomo. I'd never get my message out.

I was heartsick over this problem of fund-raising, because I didn't think there would ever be another opportunity as real as this one seemed to be. But I could not simply *run* for governor. I wanted a reasonable shot at *being* governor—not for the title, but to make a difference. I sincerely thought Cuomo's policies were bad for the state; they were slowly eroding my future, my children's future. Yes, I wanted to see him defeated, but more than that I wanted to help lead the turn-around New York desperately needed. I wasn't interested in looking back and reminiscing about my failed run for the state's highest office; with no real financial backing, and a long-standing nonaggression pact still in place between Cuomo and D'Amato, I'd be an unknow-able unknown, and the only likely scenario was that I'd be unable to win at the polls. So I turned away from a nomination that could well have been mine.

As party platform chairman I continued to travel across the state, holding hearings, meeting with local leaders, and getting myself out there. As a local politician myself, I was little known to voters outside my own district, so this was a good chance to lay a foundation for 1994, if it turned out that my chance might somehow come again—if not for governor, then for some other statewide office. Also, it was an opportunity to at least set an agenda for the 1990 gubernatorial elec-tion; if I couldn't campaign against Cuomo myself, I could throw him a few curves. We put together a great platform that year.

By the summer of 1993, with Cuomo misstepping his way through a third term, the nomination again came knocking. It was just a faint knock at first, but I was listening for it. I was a few months into my first term as state senator, and as frustrated as possible. Getting there had been frustrating enough (it took an arduous primary battle against an enormously popular incumbent, Mary Goodhue, the only Republican woman in the state senate during the vaunted Year of the Woman), but being there was proving even tougher. I was immedi-ately cast as an outsider—and my ideas were cast out with me. Good-hue left behind many friends of long standing, and none of them were happy with the way I had campaigned against her in the primary. Pri-vately, many of them had pledged their support; but as soon as I an-nounced my candidacy, virtually every one of those who'd urged me to run (including, most notably, the Westchester County GOP chair-man, Tony Colavita) left me hanging. Now that I was there, few of them wanted anything to do with me.

It had been nearly fifty years since a Republican state senator had been beaten in a primary, unless he had been convicted of a crime, and when I came along the tight circle of incumbent Republicans and Democrats seemed to close ranks against me. It was obvious that I stood as a threat, and I'm sure a great many of my new colleagues wished I'd beat a hasty retreat to the obscurity of Peekskill. But I wasn't going anywhere just yet.

For years, I'd looked on from my lowly vantage point in the assembly and wondered what happened to all our bright young Republican leaders when they moved to the senate. Colleagues of mine would campaign for a senate seat and then turn into what I half-seriously called "pod people." It was like something out of *Invasion of the Body Snatchers*, the way these good people were taken over by a system that sapped their true beliefs and transformed them into loyal, blinders-wearing members of the powerful elite. They went over believing in smaller government, lower taxes, and a redoubling of our efforts against crime, and yet year after year they ended up voting for bigger spending programs, higher taxes, and weaker criminal laws.

It happened time after time. The most dependable person on our side in the assembly would get elected to the senate and just vanish, and it took winning a senate seat myself to understand why. Every single element of a senator's ability to make an impact flowed through the senate majority leader, Ralph Marino, from Oyster Bay on Long Island; or to be more accurate, through his counsel, Angelo Mangia. Marino and Mangia were the strange and powerful forces in this particular play, making virtually all major policy decisions and then strong-arming senators into accepting them. The other senators used to refer to Mangia behind his back as the "prince of darkness"; one look at him, and you knew you could either fall in behind Marino or suffer the consequences.

Ralph Marino thought of himself as the most powerful Republican in the state. Apart from Senator Alfonse D'Amato, he probably was. But he was also an embarrassment to the party. His power (and there was no denying his influence) flowed mainly from his pointedly close ties to the Cuomo administration. It also flowed from the uniquely flawed legislative system of New York. In both the senate and the assembly, legislators had for decades ceded more and more power to their respective leaders—the speaker of the assembly and the majority leader of the senate. While in the assembly the Democrats were so overwhelmingly and hopelessly liberal that there was no hope for change, in the senate, there was no excuse. The majority of senators were good people who believed as I did. They never had the chance to vote their conscience, however, because their leader, Ralph Marino, never gave them the chance. Each leader has the power to determine all committee assignments, staff allotments, budget items, and pending legislation; indeed, it wouldn't be an overstatement to suggest that nothing passes the legislature or gets into the budget without the approval of these two men. A legislator could see his own pay supplemented by a "lulu," or extra stipend, which might reach $25,000 a year. His district could receive $2 or $3 million a year in "member items." Or a legislator could receive only his base salary and no appropriations for his district—all at the whim of one person.

This is an awesome power, sufficient to keep in line all but the most uncontrollable legislators. In Marino's case, this power was further corrupted by the close support of the opposing-party governor, who'd tacitly pledged never to help defeat any of Marino's senate allies—in exchange for which Marino helped to lead Republican senators down paths they would rather not have taken.

The alliance between Marino and Cuomo was well known—or, I should say, well suspected—but it wasn't until I moved into the executive office chamber one year later that I discovered the full extent of their ties. Marino's private unlisted telephone numbers were programmed into the speed-dial feature on what had been Cuomo's telephone. Even more telling were the flight logs left behind showing that *G-1*, the state plane, had been sent every week to Long Island to pick up Marino and Mangia and fly them to Albany, and then back again a few days later.

Stymied in my new post in the senate, I listened carefully for the next opportunity. And when the path cleared for another try for governor I jumped onto it with both feet. This time, the only obstacle would be New York senator Alfonse D'Amato. Initially, D'Amato let it be known in mid-1993 that he himself was considering a run for governor, and a late summer fund-raiser at the Sheraton in Manhattan was rife with speculation that he would soon announce his candidacy. I left the hotel after the event and crossed the street to an Irish bar called Rosie O'Grady's, to have a drink with some of my friends and advisers, including Tim Carey and Mike Finnegan.

I was fairly dejected at this latest turn, and worried once again that 1990 had been my only shot. Clearly, I couldn't go up against a party powerhouse like D'Amato, who could guarantee himself the nomination and very likely win the general election. But what was also clear was that Bill Clinton was floundering after less than one year in the White House. You didn't have to be a political guru to see that the national mood was changing, and that 1994 promised to be a good year for Republicans, just as 1992 had been a strong year for Democrats. I looked at the field and thought I'd be left out. New York could have a new governor, lieutenant governor, attorney general, and comptroller, perhaps even a new United States senator if D'Amato left his seat to go up against Cuomo. Every statewide office might turn over, and I'd still be in the state senate—or, worse, on the sidelines.

I couldn't go back to the assembly, and my frustration was such that another term in the senate was out of the question. Clearly, I lacked the money—or clout—to win the nomination for governor over D'Amato, or even lieutenant governor, and my relationships with most of my new colleagues in the senate were not likely to bring me much support.

With D'Amato still looking at it, the governor's office was apparently out of the mix, so I didn't know where I'd end up. In fact, the original bumper stickers I printed and later used in the gubernatorial campaign said "Pataki '94," because I was never quite sure which way to turn. There was some talk in party circles that if D'Amato didn't declare himself a candidate for governor, I might emerge as a workable alternative. I didn't know this at the time, but I learned it later, and soon enough. The first hint came that night at Rosie O'Grady's, when I let slip that I'd been thinking of starting an exploratory committee for the 1994 election. I was thinking out loud, fishing for opinions, and the idea found me on the rebound. We'd been joined at our table by my friend Kieran Mahoney, a great Republican strategist and consultant and a former D'Amato staffer, and he pricked up his ears. He listened as I laid out my whole strategy for 1994, and all I got back was a stare. "I wouldn't do that right now if I were you," he finally said.

"But '94 is going to be a good year for us," I countered. "I can win."

I pressed him on it, but I couldn't get Kieran to be more specific. He promised to tell me more when he could, but he was vague on when that might be.

A few days later I met D'Amato's powerful and smart communications director, Zenia Mucha, in Saratoga. "Zenia, let the senator know I'll do all I can to help him if he runs for governor," I said.

She smiled. "I don't think he's running," she said. "If he doesn't . . ." She didn't finish the sentence, but the impression was clear. Maybe opportunity does knock twice.

A couple of weeks later I got a phone call from Mahoney and Bill Powers, the new state party chairman. Powers was an ex-marine: tough, smart, and committed to rebuilding the party brick by brick. In 1993, he was working to elect GOP candidates to win across the state, and to elect Rudy Giuliani as New York City mayor. Quite simply, Bill Powers is a winner, and he was committed to seeing the GOP win all across New York—including, for the first time in twenty years, the office of governor.

"I've got Kieran with me here on the line," Powers said. "We've got something we need to tell you."

"We know you're considering running in '94," Mahoney said.

"Well, we think you're the right person to go up against Cuomo," Powers added. "You've got the right record. You're willing to stand up for what you believe in. You're the only senator to vote against Cuomo's tax increase. We think you can beat him, and we think you'll be a great governor."

I couldn't believe it. Maybe 1990 hadn't been my once-in-a-lifetime chance after all. I immediately thought of Libby and the kids. The 1992 primary and the senate election had been brutally tough. Going up against Cuomo would be even tougher, more brutal. Was it fair to put the people I love through another ordeal so soon after the one before? This would take some thinking, but I pushed this thought aside for the time being. "What about D'Amato?" I asked. "I thought he was running."

"He's not," Mahoney announced. "You're the right guy, but there's just one problem. D'Amato isn't sure he can get behind you, and his support is very important."

I knew D'Amato and I weren't always on the same page, but I thought it ended there. "So why are you calling me?" I asked, thinking that they either wanted to help or wanted to let me know why they couldn't.

"To get you and D'Amato talking," Powers said. "You should go to Washington to meet with him and get his support." The party was behind me, they said, but now I needed to get Al D'Amato's support.

Oh, I thought. That's all. Just the most influential Republican in the state. Just a man with whom I seemed to have a fundamental disconnection.

I'd always admired what Al D'Amato was able to accomplish for New York, even if we didn't always see things the same way. His tenacity was unrivaled, and when he got involved in an issue he put everything into it. He had an image as an unrefined operative, a short Italian with glasses, a product of the Nassau County machine, but his record gave the lie to his reputation. D'Amato was and remains an extremely hardworking, conscientious leader who's done more for his constituents and the state of New York than the previous six senators combined. He gets things done, but his nature is confrontational. He tends to yell. My nature is not at all confrontational. I tend not to yell. I look for common ground to get around an impasse. D'Amato bludgeons people into submission. He doesn't give up. I don't give up too easily myself, but I try to be a bit more subtle about it. We have very different personalities, and very different styles. But despite our differences in style, Al D'Amato and I have become good friends. I enjoy his company; he's funny and sincere. Nonetheless, over the years our differences made for some very uneasy situations. In 1991, when I was thinking of running for Westchester County executive, he put out the word that he'd endorse anybody except me. He was even quoted in the papers as saying, "Anybody but Pataki."

Clearly I needed to put this behind us. "I'll go see him right away," I said.

"Do it today," Mahoney said. "The election is in fourteen months. We've got work to do."

I took the afternoon off and told no one why. I had a million thoughts bouncing around my head. Was I ready? Did I stand a chance? Was this what I really wanted for my family? I raced home to catch Libby while the kids were still in school, and I laid the situation out for her. She wasn't as shocked as I was at the call.

"You're the right one," she concluded. "You can do the job. Yes, it'll be hard on us, but it's what you've always wanted."

With that kind of support and confidence, how could I say no? I flew down to Washington and met with Senator D'Amato in the Senate cafeteria. We talked about our past differences.

"We've never really gotten along," he acknowledged.

"No," I said, "but that shouldn't matter, The state's all screwed up. Cuomo's ineffective. There are all these people who want to run, but some of them have never governed. Those who've been in the Congress or the senate have all voted for one or another of Cuomo's budgets or tax increases. But I've won some tough races. My positions are solid. My record is solid."

"I don't know if I can trust you," D'Amato said. "You'll probably stab me in the back like most of the other people I've helped. But if I'm going to help you take on Mario Cuomo, I need to know that you're going to do what you say you're going to do."

I was disarmed by his candor. I soon learned that D'Amato is always candid. "Senator," I said, "I certainly understand that you win elections as a team. We need you on that team to win."

"Well," the senator finally said, "everyone I've talked with thinks you're the right person. They like what you bring to the table— your ideas, your convictions, and your determination. Most of all, they think you can win and I'm not going to let our past differences stand in the way of unseating Mario Cuomo. Let's go win the race, Governor."

It was the first time anyone had used the title with me in mind, and I wasn't ready for it. "Don't call me governor," I said. "It's bad luck."

I was ecstatic. Just a few hours ago I had been out of the loop, and now I was all the way inside. With D'Amato's influence and his ability to raise money, and with Powers's commitment to win and to bring along the state party, it all seemed too good to be true. It was.

D'Amato went to work right away. He asked me to give him a couple of days to work the phones, talk to some people, see what they thought. He wanted to form a consensus behind him quickly before publicly getting out in front. I understood that, but I wasn't expecting to hear from him just a few days later with bad news.

"We've got a problem, George," he said.

I noticed that he didn't call me governor this time. "What is it?"

"Marino," he responded. "I don't know what happened with the two of you, but he positively hates you. He will not support you under any circumstances, and the last thing I need is a fight with Marino."

"Maybe if we sat down," I tried, "talked things through a little bit."

"Look," D'Amato insisted, "there's nothing to talk about. Marino won't support you, and I'm not going to go over Marino. He says anybody but you, so I'll be honest with you. We're going to look for somebody else, and if we can come up with somebody we can all agree on, I'll go with them."

If Marino wouldn't support me, I thought, it meant that Cuomo knew I could beat him. It no doubt fell to Marino, as senate majority leader, to serve up an unelectable Republican candidate, helping to clear the way for a fourth term for his good friend Mario, and to keep his own good thing going.

I wasn't about to be abandoned by the party leadership a second time. "Well, senator," I said to D'Amato, when he told me he wouldn't go over Marino, "if that's how you see it, I understand, but I'm going to run anyway."

And I did. From that moment forward, I traveled the state, doing what I could to raise money (and my profile), meeting state committee members, talking to the press, putting myself out there. I used my vague "Pataki '94" campaign literature and stationery, but my goal was precise: I would be the next governor of the state of New York, with or without D'Amato or Marino or anyone else in the Republican Party.

People saw I was running as the "non-Cuomo" of candidates. In a campaign about ideas and policies, mine were essentially the opposite of Cuomo's. He raised taxes; I'd cut them. He let violent felons out of jail early; I'd keep them in longer. He ignored workfare; I'd make it law, and end welfare as a way of life. The differences were clear and dramatic.

All along, I had the support of Bill Powers at the head of the state party. "Marino doesn't want us to win," Powers kept assuring me. "He wants to lose and sooner or later Alfonse will realize that. Just keep going. Everything'll work out."

So I kept going. Over the next months, into early 1994, the Republican field began to take shape; I was clearly the choice among conservative Republicans. Herb London, who had run as the Conservative Party candidate for governor in 1990, emerged as the choice of those who had backed him before. Former congressman Bill Green emerged as the choice of "moderate" Republicans, the old Rockefeller wing.

Powers and Mahoney stuck fast with me, but still D'Amato and Marino kept looking. And looking. At one point, the party leaders seemed to be serving up the millionaire of the week for consideration. Every week the *Post* had a new page three headliner. David Cornstein. Donald Trump. They looked everywhere but at me. Marino let it be known that I would be the next governor "over his dead body," so Republicans floated every conceivable name (and several inconceivable names) just to measure the public reaction.

Finally, I read in the *Post* that they were looking at Frank Zarb, who had been energy secretary under President Ronald Reagan and who had recently enjoyed tremendous success as a businessman. Zarb, in fact, would have been a solid candidate and an excellent governor, but he never really considered running. Nevertheless, on the day of the *Post* report I ran into my old leader from the assembly, Clarence Rappleyea, in the hall of the state capitol. Rapp had been one of the first to set aside his own ambitions when D'Amato called and agreed, privately, to support me for governor. He could see I was dejected. "You're going to be our next governor," Rapp said, as if he had it on good authority.

"What do you mean?" I shot back. "They're looking at everyone but me. Just look at today's *Post*. They're talking about Frank Zarb."

"That's just my point," Rapp offered. "Think for a minute. They're up to 'Z' in the Rolodex."

It was a bitter joke, but dead-on. The search for a certain loser was doomed from the start. D'Amato, Powers, Rappleyea, and the rest didn't want just any candidate; they wanted a winner, and their search was proving futile. It reminded me of 1990, with D'Amato sitting it out on the sidelines in a nonaggression pact, when party leaders had actually gone through the Rolodex of state senator Roy Goodman of Manhattan, before coming up with the name of Pierre Rinfret, the eventual nominee who shall forever be remembered as the candidate who almost came in third and almost cost the Republican Party Row B. They were at it again.

As it happened, just a few days after the item about Zarb was leaked, I took a call from D'Amato confirming Rapp's hunch. "Marino's impossible," the senator said. "I can't deal with him. We can't agree on anyone. He can't get anyone to agree with him on Herb London, because London's a sure loser, and he won't look at anyone else. I want to win, so I'm going with you."

It wasn't exactly a ringing endorsement, but I wasn't about to quibble. "Wonderful, senator," I said. "Thank you. Let's go win."

The London-Marino roadblock didn't disappear, but with D'Amato's support I now had a good chunk of the mainstream party establishment behind me, and a straight shot to the convention that spring. I also had the full benefit of Alfonse D'Amato's enthusiasm. Just as he gave everything he had to issues of interest, so too did he give his all to a campaign. He made key members of his staff available to me. He worked on strategy. He raised money. He campaigned at my side; and when he wasn't with me, Bill Powers was there to show the party's support.

The goal, initially, was to win 75 percent of the convention vote and thus keep the other candidates from qualifying for a primary. Of course, every other candidate had the same goal: Herb London; the former ambassador to France, Evan Galbraith; Congressman Bill Green; and the former state party chairmen, Pat Barrett and Richard Rosenbaum. The only real threat, I thought, was London; it wasn't that I thought he could beat me (our team was too strong for that), but if he tallied 25 percent he'd qualify for a primary, and in the process land the Conservative Party nomination. I wasn't frightened by a head-to-head campaign against Mario Cuomo, and I wasn't worried about capturing the Republican nomination outright in a primary, but I did want to keep London off the ballot in November; his conservative line could siphon off hundreds of thousands of votes that would otherwise go to the Republican candidate.

The convention (and its aftermath) confirmed my suspicions regarding London's backing. A candidate far too dogmatic even for the Republican mainstream, he somehow had Marino and Mayor Rudy Giuliani—two very liberal Republicans—working actively to get him the nomination. This made no sense, unless the Cuomo camp was behind the plan, getting its Republican allies to support the one candidate who had no real chance of defeating the governor. And the effort very nearly succeeded. Marino threatened the jobs of Republican delegates who worked for the senate, and there were dozens of them.

In the end, London fell just two points shy of 25 percent—close enough that he wasn't going away without a fight. He threatened to sue, claiming we had cheated him out of his votes, and demanded a recount. It was a ridiculous charge, but he had some party heavy-weights behind him, so we tried to broker a truce. To his credit, London truly wanted to see Cuomo defeated and was reluctant to split the anti-Cuomo vote. Now it seemed that the best way to get London to back off the gubernatorial race and make him a part of the team was to run him for another statewide office.

Comptroller, it turned out, was what he wanted, but the problem with this was that John Faso, a dedicated Republican assemblyman from Kinderhook, wanted the same thing. Faso was one of the good guys, a colleague and friend of long standing, and he'd spent the past year campaigning for the nomination. By all rights, it should have been his, but it fell to me and Rapp, Faso's assembly leader, to sit with John and lay out our dilemma. We explained how his stepping aside to make room for London was the only way to bring unity to a divided party, how our objective was to change the state, how the only way to do that was to beat Mario Cuomo.

"It's a lousy deal, I know" I told him, "but if London is willing to take the comptroller race and work with us on the governor thing, we should take it."

He gave it a great deal of thought, which I certainly understood, given the tremendous sacrifices he and his family had made over the past year. "I understand," he finally said. "I'm disappointed, but I understand."

The amazing thing is that he really did understand, and what was most amazing was not that John Faso put his own ambition aside for the good of the party and the state, but that people like Ralph Marino were so willing to put their own ambitions ahead of the good of the people. There are all types of elected officials, but I'd take someone like John Faso over someone like Ralph Marino any day of the week.

We rounded out what appeared to be a strong ticket with Dennis Vacco, the former U.S. Attorney from Buffalo, and a great candidate for attorney general, and Betsy McCaughey, a think-tank analyst, for lieutenant governor. For a while, with the nomination in hand, the campaign went great. It was clear the people agreed with the ideas and policies I was outlining. They wanted violent felons behind bars; they wanted the death penalty; they wanted a welfare system that required and rewarded work, and that respected those who worked a difficult job at five dollars an hour more than the able-bodied adults who sat at home and opened their government checks; they wanted tax cuts and jobs . . . all of which we were seeking.

The theme of the campaign was simple: New York was number one in all the wrong categories; as governor, I promised to make us number one in all the *right* categories—number one in cutting taxes instead of in tax burden, number one in reducing welfare instead of welfare dependency, number one in reducing crime instead of rate of crime. At every campaign stop, I recalled my grandparents, and the hopes and goals they carried with them as they saw the Statue of Liberty for the first time after their long passage. "J. C. Penney may have moved to Texas," I would say, "and W. R. Grace may have moved to Florida, but the Statue of Liberty hasn't moved. It still stands in New York harbor. It still represents the hopes and dreams we have for ourselves, for our children and grandchildren. With the right policies, those hopes, those dreams, that belief in a better future we have for our children and families *will* come true—not in Atlanta or Dallas or Durham, but right here in New York State."

My confidence began to soar. Charlie Gargano, a good friend of Senator D'Amato's and a highly successful businessman and diplomat, joined our team to head our fund-raising effort. His results were spectacular. We were actually *outraising* Cuomo and getting our message out. And the people were listening. They believed. I could sense it in the crowds and see it in the polls. We were going to have our chance.

As I traveled the state I could tell that our message for change was catching hold. I recall one day in western New York—in Erie County, a blue-collar Democratic stronghold. I spent part of the afternoon with Senator Mary Lou Rath and Bernadette Castro, who was also campaigning for statewide office and who is now New York's outstanding parks commissioner; we were in Amherst, a suburb of Buffalo, meeting with community leaders and small business owners. They believed in our program to cut taxes. They thought we could improve the economic climate, help them to stay in business and add employees. They wanted change.

With Tom Reynolds, our leader in western New York and my close friend, and Tony Gioia, a great friend and prominent community leader, we went to some of the Italian neighborhoods on the west side of Buffalo. We walked into a deli on Grant Street, and people said, "Oh, Pataki—you're the one who wants to make welfare recipients work. I'm voting for you."

But the best indication came from Tom Reynolds's secret barometer: He sent me with Bobby Wysnewski to the bowling alleys of Cheektowaga. This largely Polish, heavily Democratic suburb of Buffalo represented swing voters across New York State. These were the old Reagan Democrats, who had embraced Reagan's patriotism and confidence in the future and left their traditional democratic roots, but who had since returned to their historic party.

"Hi, how ya doing? How are you hittin'em today?" I would ask as I shook hands with people bowling in one of Cheektowaga's many alleys.

"Oh, Pataki. I've seen your ads. You're the one who wants the death penalty. I'm voting for you." As Bobby and I worked our way down through the large group of seniors, the response was overwhelming. These voters had heard our message. They had been forced out of Buffalo to the suburbs by unacceptable rates of violent crime. They had seen their blue-collar jobs move to the South because of oppressive taxes. They had worked hard all their lives and couldn't understand how people would take advantage of their compassion and live for years on New York's failed welfare system. "We're voting for you," a soft-spoken, gray-haired lady said to me while sitting at the desk keeping score for her friends. "You're what we need."

As positive as the reception had been in Buffalo and western New York, I felt the same energy visiting in Brooklyn and on Long Island. Mike Long and Guy Molinari took me through a senior-citizen center in Bay Ridge. Time and again they would say, "Oh, Pataki—you're the one who wants the death penalty, you're the one who wants to make welfare people work, we're voting for you."

I would speak to them about my family history. About my hopes for the future. About my desire not to have to visit my children in North Carolina or Georgia. And recognition would immediately shoot into their eyes. "My daughter lives in Atlanta," one would say; "My grandchildren live outside Dallas," another would add. They understood my message, not from any deep philosophical study, but from their own experience. They felt that I was right, that we needed to change New York State, that we needed a new direction to have safer streets, to have our children living down the block instead of at the other end of the country.

And I took my message to Long Island. I campaigned across Suffolk County with the new chairman of the Suffolk County Republican Committee, John Powell, one of my earliest and strongest supporters. I said school taxes were too high, taxing too many people from their homes. I told the voters that we should, finally, use the more than $1 billion in lottery profits to lower homeowners' school taxes. They believed it. They were willing to give me a chance.

By the way, that plan is now law.

Then comes Rudy Giuliani's late-in-the-game endorsement of Mario Cuomo. Up until this time Giuliani and I had enjoyed what I thought was a decent relationship. We weren't close, but I'd worked with him on a number of initiatives, and I had always felt that our philosophies on crime and welfare and taxes were somewhat consistent.

Rudy Giuliani was a Republican mayor in a tough Democratic city. Clearly, his support would have been appreciated. And certainly it was expected. After all, how could a Republican endorse a man who wholeheartedly embraced every liberal philosophy that Republicans opposed.

In his twelve years as governor, Mario Cuomo championed and advanced every liberal cause under the sun: big government, high taxes, weak criminal laws, and a welfare system that promoted government dependency over individual responsibility.

Mario Cuomo was the antithesis of all that Republicans stood for. I felt there was no way Giuliani could endorse Cuomo.

But on October 24, the unthinkable happened. I was up in Watertown at the time, meeting with a local newspaper's editorial board. Tom Doherty stepped out to take a call, and when we boarded the plane for a rally in Rochester, I could tell by the look on Tom's face that something was wrong.

"Tom, what's doing."

"Well, Senator," Doherty began. (He knew better than to call me governor.) "Giuliani endorsed Cuomo."

I couldn't believe what I was hearing. I was shocked. This was out of the blue.

Libby and Doherty were looking at me as if they were waiting for a show of anger. But I was too shocked to be angry.

And although I was concerned about what Giuliani's bizarre endorsement would mean politically, I also knew that political endorsements are largely symbolic gestures—and as welcome as Giuliani's endorsement would have been, it wasn't going to distract me from doing what I'd set out to do.

Nor was it going to change the mood of New Yorkers, who were fed up with high taxes, high crime, record job losses, and a welfare system that was growing out of control.

Initially, the poll numbers moved in Cuomo's favor. But after several days things began to go the other way.

Giuliani's endorsement seemed to galvanize Republicans who were loyal to our principles—the principles of less government, lower taxes, and a no-nonsense approach to fighting crime. The rallies I attended after the endorsement were louder and more spirited and enthusiastic than ever.

Giuliani made the mistake of trying to campaign for Cuomo in upstate New York. But everywhere he went, Pataki supporters were waiting for him. Their chants drowned out his press conferences. In Buffalo, they outnumbered Giuliani supporters twenty to one. In Utica, there were so many Pataki supporters waiting to "greet" Giuliani that he never left the plane.

And so, what at first was bad news for the campaign turned out to be the opposite. Now the campaign gained momentum and passion. The campaign was gaining steam. Money was pouring in faster than ever. Pataki supporters were more excited and united than ever.

And despite the shocking news just a few days earlier that New York City's Republican mayor had endorsed New York's liberal, status quo governor, New Yorkers seemed more eager than ever to usher in a new era of change. We were soaring.

You could actually feel it. When you're out there on the road shaking hands you get a real sense of how the people are reacting to you. You see it in their eyes, and you hear it in their voices. It's better than polling, and if you do it often enough, and well enough, you can get a fairly accurate reading from the crowd. At first, I started to sense a real rooting interest from the people we were seeing, particularly upstate. Jack Kemp, a great leader and a good friend, came out to join me for a few appearances, and he began to sense it too. The polls were slower to respond. They showed our lead evaporate and Cuomo pull ahead by more than ten points. But I felt that the reaction we were getting would soon show up in the numbers.

One morning, about ten days out, I was due at La Guardia Airport for a press conference, with Kemp at my side. We were running late, and in my haste to get ready I cut myself shaving. No big deal, but it was six in the morning, and it was still dark, and I didn't want to wake Libby looking for a styptic pencil. I tried to dab the cut with a hand towel, to apply a little pressure, but it kept bleeding. Then, in desperation, I pinched a couple of pieces of toilet paper to blot the cut and headed out to the car.

We picked up Tom Doherty on the way, in lower Westchester. "How's it going, Tom?" I said.

"Great, senator," he replied, cheerful as always. "How are you?"

I pointed to a *Daily News* headline on the seat alongside me: "Cuomo Lead Now Double-Digit." "We're doing great, huh?" I said.

"Ignore that stuff," Tom replied.

The excitement we were feeling on the road had still not shown up in the polls. For the first time in a long year of campaigning, I started to think I might actually lose. I also started to think I might never blot away the blood from my morning shave. "We need a drugstore, Tom," I said. "I need to fix this cut. This is your town. Where should we go?"

"Senator, it's six-thirty in the morning. I don't usually go shopping at six-thirty in the morning." He directed Eddie Keegan to a store he thought might be open. "Nervous?" he asked, turning back to me.

"Me?" I joked. "I've got ice water in my veins. Besides, I've got a job offer to sell used cars in Peekskill if I lose."

"No luck here," Keegan called from the front seat. "We can try on the way to the airport."

For the rest of the drive down to the Marine Air Terminal, we kept looking for an open drugstore, but we pulled in foiled. I looked in the mirror. There was toilet paper hanging from my chin and blood seeping through. I thought about the headlines, the double-digit gap in the polls. I could see the new headline with a picture of my oozing face— PATAKI: CAN'T STOP THE BLEEDING. Altogether, it made for a pretty miserable picture. But then I smiled back at myself and thought, Hey, it couldn't get much worse.

As I barnstormed across the state, I remember one particularly exciting night. New York is different from most other states in that we have six permanent parties. By far the most important other than the Republicans and Democrats are the Conservatives. The Conservative Party was created to offset the liberalism of the GOP under Nelson Rockefeller. It is home to thousands of conservative Republicans and Reagan Democrats—blue-collar conservatives who share the same general Republican philosophy, but because of background and history are uncomfortable in the GOP.

The Conservative Party's annual preelection dinner was being held in New York, at the Marriott Marquis Hotel on Wall Street. Mike Long, a former Marine from Brooklyn and the Conservative Party chairman, is one the strongest political supporters anyone could ever have. He gave a rousing introduction at the dinner and then called on Bill Buckley to introduce me to the crowd. Buckley got up and talked about my ideas and concepts and got the crowd ready for what I feared could be my anticlimactic response. It was a large, enthusiastic audience. I could feel that they believed that this was a race that could be won. I got up and deviated from my standard speech. "You know," I told them, "there has never been a governor elected in New York State running with the Conservative line. There are those who hope there will never be a governor elected in New York State running with the Conservative line. Unfortunately, many of them are Republicans. They would rather deal with Cuomo, deal with the Democrats, deal with the Liberals, than have to face up to the tough decisions and true principles required of a conservative governor. You all know that. But you should also know something else. Their time has passed. We are going to win. There is going to be a new government. We're going to have a new direction for this state. We're going to end welfare as an entitlement and require workfare. We're going to end the lenient criminal justice policies and have the death penalty for someone who would kill our police officers. We're going to make us number one in tax cuts instead of number one in taxes. We're going to be able to visit our kids down the block, instead of across the country."

And then I got into the emotion of the moment. "You know those opposed to change, those opposed to seeing someone actually win with Conservative support, those in favor of the status quo, tried to prevent this from happening. But they made a mistake. I can tell that from this crowd. I can tell from crowds from across the state. Our cause is not getting weaker, it is getting stronger. They may have wounded me, but they could not kill our cause. We're fighting back, we're getting our message out, bringing the values we know are right for the twenty-first century all across this state. And you know what? We're going to win!"

The crowd went nuts. The energy was back. The defection of those in our own party who wanted to keep the status quo for their own reasons had failed to bring us down. But it had succeeded in one thing. It had succeeded in energizing those who shared those beliefs. It had succeeded in generating a massive turnout in conservative upstate areas. It had succeeded in mobilizing those who had taken for granted that twelve years of liberal failure, Mario Cuomo's reign, would simply come to an end. They knew now that we had to work to bring it to an end. They were prepared to do that work.

And in addition to mobilizing our base and energizing Conservative and upstate Republican voters, I had support from other corners as well. One of the more unlikely turns of the campaign was the emergence of the radio personality Howard Stern as a factor in state politics. For a time, it actually looked as if the self-proclaimed "king of all media" would oppose me as the Libertarian candidate for governor. Bright, funny and—off the air—a genuinely nice and caring guy, Howard's on-air personality had given him a huge following in New York. There was a bona-fide convention in Albany, at which he received the Libertarian Party's nomination, after which he started promoting himself on the radio, giving speeches, and raising money. He got tremendous press coverage, and he was registering ten to twelve points in the polls—an extraordinary showing for a political outsider. He campaigned on three issues: He was in favor of the death penalty; he supported nighttime construction on our roads and highways; and (a related issue) he wanted to use the ashes of executed felons to help fill in potholes. His plan, he said, was to appoint a proven administrator as his lieutenant governor, enact his three initiatives, and resign his post after making his changes, and his point.

It was exactly the sort of antigovernment platform to motivate hundreds of thousands of disaffected voters throughout the state, many of whom were devoted listeners of Howard Stern's radio program. Howard Stern spoke to those people, and they responded. He was funny and outrageous and pushy, and he was showing up as a factor in the polls. I'm certain he would have tallied in the double digits if his campaign had run through election day.

Ultimately, though, he pulled out, because of what he thought were particularly onerous financial disclosure laws. The disclosure rules are in place to safeguard the public interest, but I can certainly see how a onetime candidate from the private sector might object to some of the details that need to be made public. Stern told his backers he just couldn't see revealing all his holdings and interests, and then he threw his support to me. We agreed on two of his three issues (I'll leave it to the reader to decide which two), and I had the distinct advantage of not being Mario Cuomo. Stern's career-long nemesis and competitor on morning radio, Don Imus, had earlier come out for Cuomo, and Howard wasn't about to see things the same way.

However it happened, I was thrilled to have Howard Stern's endorsement, because I knew what it meant. I liked him. He made me laugh. I didn't necessarily want my kids to listen to his program just yet, and I was embarrassed to tune him in on the radio if my mother was in the car with me, but he was smart, insightful, and entertaining. I went on the air with him a few times, during what was left of the campaign, and he was always respectful and well-prepared. He knew politics, and he knew people. Libby went on too, and she had a fine time, fending off his questions about her love life, and his support and general enthusiasm were instrumental in our campaign. I don't know how to quantify it, but he definitely made an impact.

All I had to do was walk through Penn Station on election night to measure his influence. It was all around. Every other comment, it seemed, had to do with Howard Stern. For everyone who said, "You'll do a great job," someone else said, "Howard told me to vote for you."

"You're going to be the next governor."

"Stern rules!"

"Down with Cuomo!"

"If we can't have Howard, you're the next best thing."

I soaked it all in and thought back once more to my childhood. If my world was about to change so dramatically, as I was by now convinced, I wanted to put things on pause for a while and consider how things had been.

5

The Values of a
Peekskill Farmer

WE WERE ALWAYS OUTSIDE, ALL YEAR LONG. EVEN WHEN there was no work to be done (and for us kids in winter, there wasn't), we refused to go inside. We had the beautiful Hudson Valley, one of the most scenic and varied regions in the northeast, as our playground. If it was freezing cold, we went ice skating; if it was snowing, we went sledding; if it was dry and sunny, we went hiking in the woods.

Most of the time, we played basketball. Winters were actually ideal for basketball on the Pataki farm. We played on a patch of dirt between my house and my cousin Bobby's house, using a crooked hoop with no net and three or four wooden planks my father had nailed up for a backboard, and when the ground was frozen the ball bounced sure and true. It was solid. You could dribble. Spring was probably the worst time of year to play, because during the thaw the ground would soften, what snow was left would start to melt, and the yard would turn to mud.

The only way to get a game in, under these conditions, was to collect some of the hay from my grandfather's cherished haystacks and pad it down atop the mud. We tried everything, and this was what worked best. We'd play for five or six minutes until the straw was mashed down into the mud, and then we'd stop and lay down some more. We'd go through a dozen applications in just a couple of hours, and we'd be covered with mud from head to foot, but it was too warm not to play.

We must have been a sight. One afternoon, a friend of my father's came by from downtown and couldn't get over how we looked. "Jesus Christ!" he exclaimed. "It's like you're in a pigpen."

He was right, I suppose; we probably looked pathetic, but it was the only court we had, and we worked it to advantage. I had one spot, off to the side, from which I never missed. The rim tilted forward and sideways, and from some angles I was almost shooting down on the basket: It was the home court advantage to end all home court advantages. Two-on-two was our game, and when we were in junior high all the big stars from the high school came down to give Bobby and me a run. Actually they came to see Bobby's sister, Judy, who was a cheerleader. But they would also play us. You had to be pretty good or pretty lucky to beat us, and few people ever did.

On hot summer days, the court kicked up too much dust to play for very long, so we retreated to the baseball field at the local elementary school. We couldn't always get enough kids together for a full-fledged game, so we played the baseball equivalent of half-court: If you were right-handed, you couldn't hit to right field; we used imaginary runners; we did whatever we had to do to make a game of it.

Sometimes, Bobby and I made a game out of nothing at all. When you grow apples, as we did, there's a phenomenon called the June drop. An apple tree, if you trim it right and pollinate it right, can set as many as five or six times the apples it intends to hold through picking season, and each June our trees dropped four or five apples for every one that stayed on. This, for us, yielded a windfall of baseballs. We gathered these little apples by the bushel, found a stick that was close to the right size, and whittled it down and rounded it off so that it looked more like a cricket bat than a baseball bat. And then we played ball. You could really hit the skins off of those things, and the apples would just mash and scatter. You could tell how well you were swinging by the way the apple splattered, and by the great *ha-thwong!* it made when you hit it square. And you could almost taste the juice in the air. It was all around.

Winters were about the best time of all. There was nothing like waking up in the middle of the night and going out for a walk in the middle of the first snowfall of the season. Ah, it was so beautiful! And quiet! There were no cars, no people, no sounds but the quiet accumulation of snow against tree, snow against ground, snow against snow. The noise of the world was swallowed up by all that snow. We'd hike up the hills surrounding our valley, or down past the reservoir, making fresh tracks into the woods on what we used to call Raccoon Hill. Sometimes we'd build a small hut, to warm us against the wind—or, if we were feeling particularly ambitious, a small fire.

One of our favorite winter pursuits was crack the whip, and the thrill of it was in the ride and in the fact that it was forbidden. My Italian grandparents had a small pond on their farm, adjacent to our property, and it doubled as our skating rink. The neighborhood kids were mostly cousins, but there were a few kids around from other families, and we all counted the days each winter until the ice was thick enough to hold us. We wore each other's hand-me-downs—skates, mittens, hats, parkas. My father joined us whenever he could, and he was the ringleader of the group. He had a mischievous streak, which sometimes ran counter to my mother's straight and narrow. She was always telling us to be careful out on the pond: Don't get hurt, don't climb the walls, don't do this, don't do that. And always, as we trundled out the door in our warm handed-down winter clothes, she shouted her final rule: Don't play crack the whip.

In crack the whip, you make a long line, join hands, and skate across the pond as fast as you can. Then you start to pivot, like a kick line in a Broadway show, and the last kid on line gets whipped across the pond at tremendous speed, as if shot out of a cannon. My father was usually the first "kid" at the end of our line. Once, on a day when the ice was a little too thin to handle all of us, we whipped my father over to where the pond wasn't fully frozen and he fell into the water. We dragged him right out, but he was drenched and freezing, and he was sick for the next few days. About the only real danger he was in, though, was that he lost his glasses in the water and couldn't see very well until he had them replaced—and that he had to shoulder my mother's disapproval when we dragged him back into the house.

They were a wonderful match, my parents, despite their contrary approaches. My father, Louis Pataki, worked even harder than he played: nonstop, full-tilt, all-out, and all the time. He worked longer than the sun. He was up before dawn, every day, readying the farm for my grandfather, doing what needed to be done, and then he was off to do his shift at the post office; in the evening he finished up around the farm and looked ahead to the next morning's work, until well past dark. Sometimes, during picking season, he even hired himself out to other farms, to earn extra money. Winters he'd moonlight at night and weekends helping my uncle Emil at a restaurant where he was a cook. I've never seen a person work half as hard as he did, or achieve half the results. He took tremendous pride in his work, and he was better and quicker at it than anyone else.

Dad wasn't running himself ragged just to make a living; it was to make a living and also to help out my grandparents. By the time I was born, in 1945, he was doing most of the work around the farm, and it remained that way until my grandfather's death in 1970 (at the age of ninety-one), but my father never took a penny out of the place. Those pennies were for his parents, and that's about what they were: Even in good years, there was hardly any income until the strawberries and cherries came in, toward the end of June; and the money stopped coming by the end of October, when the apples were through.

It wasn't money but my father's sense of family and responsibility that kept him working at Grandpa's side. How it fell to him, and not to any of his siblings, was never entirely clear. Most likely, he took it on himself, although it was equally likely that he took it on himself because there was no one else. There was my aunt Zelma, my cousin

Bobby's mother, and she and her husband always helped out, but Uncle Fred worked in New Jersey and was usually gone twelve hours a day. There was Uncle John, who was born in Hungary, but he worked as an engineer building ships for the Navy; though he still lived on the farm, he was generally in Washington and home only on weekends. Uncle George, the baby of the family, went to college (a Pataki first) and then joined the Army, and his path took him even farther afield. He went off to fight in the Far East, married a Filipino woman, and never really came back to the farm for anything more than a short visit. He retired a full colonel and settled in California, where he made a decent amount of money in real estate (another Pataki first).

And then there was Uncle Elmer, whose name I also carry; he was diagnosed with amyotrophic lateral sclerosis, about a decade after Lou Gehrig suffered through its final stages, so he of course couldn't work on the farm. Ironically, he was the biggest and strongest of all, in a big and strong family, but the disease left him unable to work at all. A hardworking Hungarian like my grandfather had trouble with my uncle's illness. We all knew the meaning of work. It was our strongest value. Even Elmer knew, and yet the ethic was so deeply held that Grandpa couldn't look at his own son, ravaged by this deadly disease, without thinking of him as someone who should be working more. To Grandpa, if you weren't working you weren't worth anything, and a part of him looked on Uncle Elmer's not working in just this way. It was a shame, and a sadness, but that was how it was.

This left my father, and Dad made it his duty to fill in the gaps when Grandpa was no longer able to manage on his own. He was younger and stronger, and it was expected. He expected it of himself. He was the son. It wasn't discussed. If you lived on a farm, you helped your parents. It was what you did—or at least it was what my father did. There was never any resentment or any question that things should be any different.

My father lived to work. It didn't matter if he was working for himself or for someone else. Even his vacations were about work. When I was a kid, we used to spend one week each summer visiting a high school friend of my mother's on Long Island, and it turned out that the woman's brother was a professional clammer, so Dad spent ten-hour days raking clams by the bushel, just to help him out. Dad wouldn't take any money, but he couldn't sit still. Even in his old age, on a trip to Hawaii with my mother near the end of his life, he was up at four o'clock in the morning, wanting to help the hotel cleanup crew water the plants and mop the floors. It was something to do, and it needed doing.

It was very clear, early on, that even if there was enough work to be done on the farm, there certainly wasn't enough profit. Dad would have to find some other way to make a living. When my father was a teenager, his older brother John was running the Hudson Grill, a twenty-four-hour diner in downtown Peekskill, and he put Dad to work as a dishwasher and short-order cook. It was exactly the sort of hard, labor-intensive work Dad loved—and it would soon yield a substantial bonus. It was while working for my uncle that Dad met my mother, Margaret Lagana, who went by the name of Peggy and worked at the Hudson Grill as a waitress. That she was there at all was as unlikely as my parents' meeting and falling in love. She had received a full scholarship to Cornell at the beginning of the Depression, but she didn't go because her father was out of work and she was the only one with a steady job. She had been number two in her high school class (although the running family joke was that there were only four students in her class, so her rank wasn't all that impressive), but she was stuck working the midnight shift at the Hudson Grill.

They decided to get married, but not before my father could find a job with long-term prospects. This was all-important to a young man of my father's way of thinking; he couldn't get married without some kind of career. The Hudson Grill was fine, but it was his brother's career, not his. After several months, my father heard of an opening at the post office. Actually, there were two openings, and he wasn't the only one looking. It was the height of the Depression, and the post office had more than 500 applicants for the two jobs. My father studied day and night for an exam the post office had prepared, the results of which would presumably narrow the applicant pool. He was determined to do well. He was working the midnight-to-ten shift with my mother, and she'd grill him on the questions and make sure he did his reading. He used to say she was the best teacher he ever had; she used to say he was a stubborn pupil. Either way, things were slow during the overnight shift, so they had plenty of time to study.

On the day of the test, my father was ready, and after the results were posted he raced back to the diner.

"Tell me," my mother said, anxious to know if her future was about to begin. "Tell me." She could see by the frown on my father's face that things hadn't gone well.

The second-highest mark out of the 500 was scored by my father's best friend and coworker at the Hudson Grill, Joe Viravic. My father had come in first.

"I scored the highest mark on the test," he said, "but I don't think I'll take the job."

"What do you mean, you won't take the job?"

"I don't think I can do what they're asking me to do."

Mom was confused. "What are they asking you to do?" she wondered.

Dad explained how he'd been visited by the head of the local Democratic Party, who told him he had to be a registered Democrat to get the job. "I know it's a good job," he explained to my mother, "and I know we need the money, but I just can't take the job like that. I'm not a Democrat. I'm not a Republican. I'm an American. They can't tell me what party to join. It's just wrong, and I don't even care about politics."

In truth, he didn't, at least not with respect to party loyalties, and my mother seemed to share his indignation. "You're absolutely right," she said. "They can't do that. It's a matter of principle. You'll find something else."

Then he left, to look for the next opportunity, leaving my mother to think of what might have been.

Later that night, he came back to the diner, wearing a smile instead of a frown. My mother knew something was up. "Say hello to Peekskill's newest Democrat," he announced proudly.

My mother beamed. "Thank God," she said. She hadn't wanted to tell my father what to do, but she was thrilled that he went out and did it on his own.

It was a lousy thing, to be strong-armed into joining the Democratic Party in order to get a job, and I would feel the same way if it had been the Republicans. Yes, from a policy standpoint of course it makes sense for government leaders to surround themselves with like-minded individuals in positions of authority. You have to do that, or be sabotaged by the holdover bureaucracy. But policy positions are far outnumbered by the nuts-and-bolts responsibilities of government; and when it comes to the regular workers and the front-line professionals who actually get the jobs done, performance should be the criterion. Throughout my career, whenever possible, I've tried to promote from within, to reward those career-committed individuals who have come up through the ranks. The first opportunity I had as mayor to appoint a judge, I reappointed a sitting Democrat. He was a good judge, of long standing, and I thought he was better qualified than any of the Republicans submitted to me for consideration. I drew some criticism from party leaders, for tapping a Democrat with my first appointment, but I didn't care. He was the right man for the job.

My father, though, had no trouble with his decision. He continued to vote his conscience—or, in some years, not at all. And he loved being a mailman. It became his pride and his passion, and I loved being a mailman's son. Before I was old enough to go to school, Mom and I used to go up Howard Hill to meet him for lunch—not every day, but most summer afternoons. We'd find a tree, in an area where there were no houses, and we'd sit and eat and talk. Dad always brought me a piece of candy from one of the merchants downtown. He knew everyone in Peekskill, and everyone knew his routine, and part of that routine meant bringing a candy for lunch with Georgie.

At the post office, Dad started out as a floater, which meant he didn't have his own route. Whenever someone was sick, or on vacation, my father would fill in. He learned the names and addresses of literally everyone in town. It got to the point where when I brought friends back to the house, I'd introduce them and he'd say, "You live at 1322 Main Street," or, "You live at 492 Simpson Place."

My mother knew everyone as well, but not because of Dad's job. She was just always friendly and open. On those walks to Howard Hill and back, she stopped and said hello to everyone. She knew people's names, and how things were with their families, and some little piece of news or innocuous gossip to pass along. It was more than simple courtesy with her. She genuinely cared for her neighbors. I try to be that way, even today, following my mother's example. I say hello to people, and not because I'm a politician. Mom wasn't a politician. People deserve to be acknowledged, she often said. Of course, I lived in New York City for a while, and I know it's rather impractical to say hello to everyone there, but certainly in Peekskill it wasn't; my mother made sure of that.

By the time I graduated from high school, Dad had been made foreman of all the mail carriers, and he would go on to become assistant postmaster; but when I think of him now, in that job, he is out on the street, in his uniform, delivering the mail, in all kinds of weather. When I was old enough, he helped me get a summer job as a letter carrier, filling in for one of his coworkers, and I remember delivering the mail and thinking what it was like for my father, all those years. Walking the route was hard enough, but he also put in a full day at the farm, and he did it all with dignity and enthusiasm.

And that wasn't all. He was also a Cub Scout leader and an active volunteer fireman. He was the first Peekskill resident to captain two different fire companies. Dad was devoted to the fire department. In fact, he was so passionate about it that he was banned from city council chambers after a dispute between the government and the volunteer firefighters. The mayor of Peekskill, Salvatore Gambino, was trying to break with tradition and control the staffing at the two volunteer fire companies in town, but the volunteers weren't about to let politicians run their operations. My father's voice was especially loud in protest at an open hearing on the matter, to the point where he was actually removed from the building. Mayor Gambino had the police drag him out, and it wasn't until I was sworn in as mayor more than a decade later that he returned. Of course, Mayor Gambino wasn't long in the office himself. He was voted out in the next election, principally because of his ill-advised (and unsuccessful) manipulation of the fire departments. My father never let the matter slide: No one messed with his fire department, not even the mayor.

We lived within the city limits, but so far out of town we couldn't hear the fire whistle. The siren was set up on top of the fire station, on Park Street. Dad arranged it so that someone would call out to the farm if the alarm sounded. He never missed a fire or a false alarm. He started out with Columbian Hose, the working-class, mostly Italian company in town, but after a while he was called in by the Cortland Hook and Ladder Company to help fight the high fires. He was fearless. He spent so much time on ladders in our apple trees—holding on with one hand, picking apples, never worrying about falling—that the hook and ladder was easy. Others would try, but the ladder wasn't affixed to anything and it swayed back and forth so violently that most of the volunteers would just freeze and climb right back down. It was simply hanging in the air.

But Dad was used to it, and up to the challenge. He was always up to the challenge. For a long time, we kept a picture from the front page of the *Peekskill Star*, the morning after a big fire at the A&P supermarket, and in the picture you could see my father, hanging on at the end of the big aerial ladder, directing the hose down on the flames. It was a two-man job, but he was the only on the ladder.

I'll never forget the Silver Lake Dairy fire, down on Main Street. It was a devastating fire, and a huge excitement to us kids. It was a Sunday evening, late, and not much was going on. We were playing baseball when someone hurried onto the field to tell us the dairy was on fire. We all ran downtown to a hill, about a block away from the dairy, where we knew we would get the best view. The dairy was housed in a four- or five-story building, and there were flames jumping out of the windows, and great black smoke was billowing up into the dusk.

After a while, one of the kids pointed out that Robinson's Paint
Store was next door, and that there would be colossal explosions if the
paint caught fire. This we knew from chemistry class, and from some
unsanctioned backyard experimenting, and from our feverish imaginations. Someone else speculated that the damage would be so great
they might have to cancel school. We were all just kids, electrified by
the fire, but I knew my father was there on the roof of that building. There were about 200 people battling that blaze, but if there was
one person on the roof it would have been my father. He was always
the first one in, the last one out, the one on the roof.

The paint store never did catch fire, and the flames at the dairy
were eventually brought under control, but at the time I was scared to
death. I tried to play it cool and not let on, but I couldn't understand
the excitement of the other kids. Their fathers were undoubtedly out
there too, but I knew mine would be on the roof. I knew that if the
paint store blew up, my father would most likely be killed. And he
knew it too. The only difference was that he wasn't afraid. I was two
blocks away, and petrified, and he was in the middle of it, doing what
had to be done.

I didn't necessarily inherit my father's fearlessness in the face of
physical danger, but he did pass on his love of learning and reading.
Oh, how I loved to read! I graduated from my Disney comics and
Landmark histories to whatever it was my brother Lou was reading in
high school. There was always a book at my bedside, facedown on the
page I'd been reading when I was called away by some other excitement, or by sleep. One of my favorite books, as a young man, was Ken
Kesey's *Sometimes a Great Notion,* and what I responded to, I think,
were the similarities between the Pataki farm and the family logging
business at the center of Kesey's story. In many ways, my family was
our regional equivalent—the old curmudgeon lumberjacks, out of
touch with what was happening; and we old, set-in-our-ways Hungarians, trying to run a turn-of-the-century European farm on a rock pile
in the middle of a city in Westchester County.

For all his grit, my father was never able to understand our place in
the culture of Peekskill. His father never understood it, either. It's a

wonder we kids were able to get by. It fell to my brother and me and our cousins to help the family assimilate, and we weren't always successful. For ourselves, we could always find acceptance on the athletic field. Sports were a tremendous leveler, then as now. It didn't matter if you had money, or if your father held one of the prestigious jobs in town, as long as you could run or hit or shoot.

Hobbies were another way into the larger community, and we pursued ours with almost competitive zeal. Ham radio was almost like a sport on our farm. My cousin Fred, Bobby's older brother, got into it first, and he sold my brother, Louis, and pretty soon Bobby and I were sold as well. We talked to people all over the world, or just to each other, across the farm. With a two-meter antenna we could talk throughout Peekskill and the Hudson Valley, and occasionally, when the skip was right, we could talk to Connecticut or New Jersey. With twenty meters, you could talk around the world. We talked to people in the Soviet Union. We talked to Cuba all the time. I once talked to someone in Africa, in Sierra Leone. We didn't say much, beyond small talk about the weather or the kind of equipment we were using, but the challenge was in making contact.

My father was happy to help us along in our interests, and he put a telephone pole in our backyard, on which we installed a giant twenty-meter beam. The pole is still there, covered with wisteria, but the antenna is no longer operational; at least the wisteria is gorgeous. I look up and remember how crazy we all were with our radios. It was a real obsession. Our rigs looked like something out of a mad scientist's lab; my brother's desk was covered with transmitters and receivers and oscilloscopes and Morse code keys; Freddy and Bobby had their attic crammed with every piece of low-end used equipment they could find; resistors, I remember, used to cost us a penny.

Every summer, we entered a VHF transmitting contest, or field day, to see how many contacts we could make in how many different regions. The snag with these contests was that you had to be mobile. It was considered cheating to participate from your rig at home, so we were constantly in search of high, open spaces where we could set up our portable antennas. We knew we'd never win, because we had poor slapped-together equipment. And we were just kids. There were a lot of serious adults at it, and they could afford to run a thousand watts of power, which was the maximum; if we had twenty watts' capability, it was a miracle.

One of our more curious field day operations took us to the top of nearby Mount Taurus—or Bull Hill, as it was known to us kids. Bull Hill, which is just north of Cold Spring, is the highest point in the Hudson Highlands, and it seemed to us about the best we could do. We were always jealous, during these contests, when we heard people broadcasting from the top of Slide Mountain. We had no idea where it was, but the name would always come booming in on our sets, and we'd be out in the backyard, on a measly hill, listening enviously. This time, though, we thought we'd really compete, and we lugged all our equipment to the top of this mountain. There was no road, and it was about a two-mile trek, most of it very steep and all uphill. We had no traditional power source, because we couldn't afford a generator, so we dragged four or five car batteries with us. We also dragged along our friend Dickie Jackson, who had no interest in ham radios but was always ready for an adventure. We needed the extra set of hands.

The hike was almost straight up, and it took two trips. On the first trip we took the transceiver, the beam, and most of the other equipment. We also took some food and water and provisional camping supplies. We planned to sleep out atop Bull Hill for the entire weekend during the contest. Then we went back down the hill to see about the car batteries. We each lifted one and realized there was no way we could carry them back to the top, so we borrowed a wheelbarrow and figured we could push them up. Of course, the path to the top was all rock and dirt, and in the end we were able to push the wheelbarrow for perhaps the first hundred yards of a two-mile trek. It took just short of forever.

That second climb was a blur, although I remember breaking into fits of uncontrollable laughter at the thought of what we looked like. There were outcroppings every now and then that overlooked the Hudson, and across the river we could see Storm King Mountain. There was a lookout across the way, where tourists could put a nickel or a dime in a viewfinder telescope and look out over the mountains and highlands. It was almost always a majestic site, except on this one afternoon, when they would have seen these three scraggly idiots carrying a wheelbarrow filled with car batteries three-quarters of the way up the highest peak.

Being brilliant theoreticians, we figured that the car batteries would work—and they would have, if they had been charged and regenerated by a running car. We didn't think about that. We got to the top of the mountain and set up our rig and started transmitting, but after about an hour the power needle dipped to zero and we were out of the running. For a moment, we had thought we would win the contest: We could hear broadcasts from along the entire East Coast; we were totally powered up; our signal was clear; we were at the highest point in the valley, looking down on Manhattan. But then we went dead, and there was nothing to do but kick ourselves over such a half-baked strategy.

We also didn't think of the rattlesnakes. Back then, there were rattlesnakes throughout the highlands. One showed up right in our path, as we were on the way up with the batteries, and we couldn't get it to move. Bobby started flailing at it with a stick, grabbed it the wrong way, and threw it up in the air. We could hear the thing rattling above our heads as we fled for cover.

All that night, in the dark, we heard (at least in our imaginations) the rattlers in the woods around us. We were sure the snakes would attack us if we slept, so we kept watch. It was miserable. We were freezing and tired, frightened by the rattlesnakes and frustrated at the opportunity squandered. It was one of the worst nights of my life. Finally, one of us had the bright idea of encircling our camp with a line of mustard, thinking the rattlesnakes would be put off by the smell and leave us alone, or at least be slowed by the thickness of the stuff. This was our stroke of genius; I don't know that it worked, but we all made it through.

My father didn't have time for sports or hobbies or crazy misadventures. Assimilating into our surrounding community may have been essential for us kids, but it wasn't part of his frame of reference.

All it was, really, was understanding the tone and tenor of the community, and working it to fit our own circumstances. Dad didn't have the patience for such subtleties, and his impatience showed. One of the facts of life on a farm is that you lose a certain percentage of your crop to local wildlife. In Peekskill, however, the local wildlife included a sizable number of adolescent vandals. "Vandals" may be too harsh a term; in Grandpa's day, they would have been called knaves; to me, back then, they were just kids, and they came from all over town to steal our cherries. My cousin Bobby and I, if we were around, tried to scare them off with our shotguns. It was a benign sort of prankishness, and I'm sure the kids thought it was all in good fun, but we did have to protect our cherries. We really had to shoot, or the kids would have just doubled back and taken their fill, so we sent a couple of rounds of buckshot over their heads and into the trees. Once they heard the branches breaking, they ran.

One year, we had spectacular cucumbers. Every once in a while, Dad's penchant for planting early extended beyond tomatoes to include cucumbers, squash, beans . . . whatever he thought he could get away with. But the months of March and April can be brutal in the Hudson Valley, and year after year Dad's crops would be wiped out by the frost. It was how things always were on our farm, until one spring when his cucumbers survived. He was thrilled, and tended those vines as if they held his own children.

Sure enough, a group of kids came by one night that spring and tore up Dad's precious cucumber vines, and when he went out that morning and saw the damage, he was absolutely livid. He was so upset he went down to the police station, before breakfast, dragging the cucumber vines with him. He must have made an incongruous picture, and yet his ethics left him no choice but to do what he did. He felt frustrated and violated, and he wanted to punish those responsible. Nothing was more important, and I watched him set off, feeling in my heart how right he was in his resentment, but knowing in my head that no one else would see it that way.

When he got to the police station, the officer at the desk looked at

my father as though he were crazy, dragging torn cucumber vines into a police station and claiming that this petty adolescent mischief was a crime. But to my father there was nothing petty about the incident, and it showed what a gap there was between his value system—rooted literally in a more rural and European lifestyle—and the values of an inner-city culture on the outskirts of New York City in the 1960s. Peekskill may have been a sleepy town of great natural beauty and shared purpose when my grandparents first descended on it at the turn of the century, but during my high school years it was like any other overgrown urban community. There was drug use; there was racial unrest. We were only a short drive from New York City, which had violent crime and an urban blight that seemed destined to reach us before too long. All around us, the world was changing, but time had stood still on the Pataki spread. It was the same mind-set that had made my grandfather stubbornly refuse to give up his horse-and-wagon delivery route, long after modern highways should have forced him off the road; here, my father and grandfather persevered in thei simple, timeless ways, while the lives around them went off in ever conceivable direction.

This gap showed itself in a variety of ways, especially in the way shaped us children. Despite our best efforts, we never really fit in. Th wasn't necessarily a bad thing—I wouldn't trade my childhood f anyone's—but these differences marked a way of life for us. We nev went to parties or hung out with the crowd at the soda fountain. ' were social outcasts, even in Peekskill, the most down-and-out co munity in the Hudson Valley. The lowest thing you could be call back then, was a Peekskill farmer. It was the most pejorative slur, cause there weren't any farms in Peekskill, except ours and the next door. There had been more farms, once, but we were the (ones holding on to that way of life; and the taunt was passed d from one generation to the next, so that finally, in my time, to Peekskill farmer was to be a backwoods hick with an outhouse. kids whose fathers worked at the railroad, or at the Fleischmann' tory, were the social elite. We never came close to that.

In some respects, this differentiation had to do with money, but there was more to it. When I was in high school, and nominated for class president, my opponent came up to me and bluntly declared what a shame it was that I had to lose. There was no rancor in his voice, but there was no respect either. He just assumed, because his father had a good job and we Patakis were simple Peekskill farmers, that he was more entitled to victory.

I was a geeky kid in high school; but there were a lot of geeky kids in our high school, and they liked me. Also, there was a significant black population in Peekskill at the time, just as there is today; and the black kids liked me too. We were all social outcasts together, and there were enough of us to get me voted in. It turned out there were more of us outsiders than insiders, a good early lesson to learn. I was flabbergasted but thrilled to have the chance to put my opponent in his place. I didn't get many chances like that.

School spirit ran high in Peekskill. There was even an organized "school spirit week," which led to perhaps the most embarrassing moment of my young life. The idea, during school spirit week, was that you dressed up for school. It was all very rah-rah and all-American. I had a tie, but I didn't have the money (or, frankly, the need) for a sports coat, so my parents arranged for me to borrow one from the son of one of their friends. This kid had graduated two years earlier, and he was relatively short and fat, while I was very tall and thin, and I stood there in the gym at lunchtime in his ill-fitting coat, wishing the day would hurry up and finish so I could run home and get into my own clothes.

Before this could happen, though, I had to face some of the guys. A group of them started pointing at me from across the gym and laughing.

"Hey, Pataki!" one of them shouted. "That's the worst-looking coat I've ever seen."

It probably was, although I didn't need to hear it. I turned away and tried to hook up with my fellow outcasts, but this guy was persistent. He reached for my collar. He wasn't menacing so much as he was

jeering. "That can't be your coat," he said. "Who did you borrow it from?" He was determined to find out, and when he finally discovered the kid's name on the inside pocket, he called it out for the benefit of his buddies. Everybody laughed, and I wanted to crawl inside a hole and hide; instead, I pretended to laugh along.

With my own group of friends, though, or with my cousins, money was never an issue, because none of us had any. We all used to go down to Huff's store after track practice and scrape together enough for an orange juice or a chocolate milk. We helped each other out with our pennies; if you had a little extra one day, you covered the guy who was short. The kids whose fathers worked at the railroad or the Fleischmann's factory had three or four shirts instead of one or two, and they ordered Huff's fifteen-cent chocolate milk instead of the five- or ten-cent version, but I didn't mind being with the have-nots.

Dad couldn't grasp why the rest of the world didn't see things the same way they seemed to him on the farm, and this was never more apparent than when my brother applied to college. Lou was four years ahead of me in school, and he had it in his head to go to Yale. I wanted to go to Notre Dame, because we always rooted for their football team, but Lou wanted to go to Yale. When he came home from school one day, his letter of acceptance was waiting for him. He opened it and saw that he hadn't received any scholarship or financial aid, and he started to cry.

"Why are you crying?" my father asked.

"Because I really wanted to go to Yale," Lou said, "and we can't afford it."

"What about a scholarship?" my father wanted to know, quite reasonably. Lou had been a National Merit Scholar, and he was eligible for scholarships at several fine schools.

"Yale isn't giving me a scholarship," Lou said.

My father, I'm sure, couldn't see why they were having this discussion. "Well, then, of course we can't afford it," he said. "I'm a mailman. If you don't have a scholarship, you can't go to Yale."

Lou got over his disappointment and accepted a scholarship from

Union College. We even drove up for a visit and stopped in at the campus store to buy his campus blazer. He was all set to go, but then we noticed in our newspaper at home that a boy from a nearby school had been considering a full scholarship from Cornell and a combination work-loan scholarship offer from Yale.

Lou showed the article to my father, and Dad was incensed. He didn't say a word to any of us, but he drove up to New Haven the next morning and went to the Yale University admissions office. He went in his work clothes, without an appointment. Everybody there was in a suit and tie. He didn't know that you had to wear a suit and tie and make an appointment. He just knew that something wasn't right about the way they were treating his son, so he sat and waited until someone would see him.

Finally, an admissions officer approached him. "Why are you here?" he asked.

My father showed him Lou's letter of acceptance, and his application. "You admitted my son," he said. "I suppose you did this because you thought he was a good student, and you want him here. But you didn't give him any scholarship." He gave the man a moment to look over the papers. "I'm a mailman," he continued. "You people are supposed to be smart, but you admit someone who clearly can't afford your tuition and you don't even offer him a scholarship. It says right here on his application how much money I make. It makes no sense."

He was right—his farmer's logic made more sense than Yale's convoluted admissions formulas. The admissions officer offered my brother a work-loan-scholarship package right there, and that's how Lou ended up at Yale. Indirectly, I suppose, that's how I ended up at Yale, too. I went because Lou went. My parents loved the school, and the education Lou was getting, and the fact that the administration had been so responsive to our particular needs, but I wasn't very excited about the prospect. I still wanted to go to a big-time football school—not to play (I wasn't any good), but to cheer—but we Patakis were Yale men now. At least, Lou and my father were Yale men. I just thought the buildings were really old, and I couldn't understand why there were vines growing up and down the outside walls. On the farm, my grandfather would have trimmed those vines back.

His methods may have been unorthodox, but my father's logic was impeccable. That's how it often was around our house. Dad was headstrong and opinionated, slightly out of step with the times. He didn't understand how organizations worked; he didn't follow established routines. Protocol was a word he'd have had to look up in the dictionary. He went about things his own way, and he usually came back with results.

I used to think my father would not have been happy in Peekskill had he known how things were for his children in terms of social status, but I realize now that it would not have mattered. It would have made no sense to him that we shouldn't enjoy the same standing and privileges as anyone else in the community. That was a notion he would have rejected. After all, he worked hard. We all worked hard. And we took pride in doing the best jobs we possibly could—in school, in sports, on the farm—which meant that in his eyes we were entitled to the same treatment as any hardworking doctor or lawyer or factory worker.

Peerksill in many ways was a model community. I grew up with an absolute sense of security. It was a safe time, and a safe place. Things are different now, but back then our religious, racial, ethnic, or economic divisions were far more subtle than they are today. It was a blue-collar town, in a blue-collar period in our history, and yet I didn't see things in terms of black and white, or rich and poor. Understand, Peekskill wasn't an elite community. It wasn't homogenized. It was a very diverse group, living under close, economically harsh circumstances, with an unshakable understanding that violence was unacceptable, and that racism or prejudice of any kind was not tolerated. We weren't blind—violence and racism were there, too—but this kind of trouble didn't find us at home.

I know it makes me sound somewhat simple and saccharine to make such a claim, but when I was a kid I never even noticed the differences among our friends. I didn't see black or white, and I tried not to see rich or poor. I looked for trust and respect and commitment. Everything else was irrelevant.

The only racial tension I experienced occurred in the affluent suburb of Chappaqua, and it too was mostly talk. It was an isolated incident, limited to a few individuals, but it affected me deeply and I remember it to this day. We were playing basketball in the Chappaqua gym, and our high school team was about half black; Chappaqua's team was all white, and a half-dozen or so kids in the Chappaqua crowd started yelling some of the most hateful, hostile invective I'd ever heard: "Niggers go home," "Go back to Harlem," and so forth.

My teammates were my friends, and the taunts cut right through me. Then these few kids started throwing things at us: bottles, garbage, newspapers. They were drunk, I guess. I didn't recognize it as a dangerous situation, but it was certainly ugly, the kind of ugliness that takes on added significance when you're in the middle of it.

Our coach, John Moro, pulled the team off the court and into the locker room. Then he went back out and told the referee and the opposing coach that our team would not put up with that kind of bigotry and racism; we would just leave.

The offenders were removed from the stands, and we went out to finish the game, but the tension in that gymnasium remained thick enough to taste. There was no more garbage throwing or name calling, but from that point on, it was clear that the crowd was *against* us, as much as it was *for* the home team. It would be nice to recall that the mood of the room changed once the few drunk kids had been tossed out, but I don't remember it that way. The fans were against us for the rest of the game, and they were against us because we came from the wrong side of the tracks, because we stood with blacks as well as with whites, because they saw in us how far we had come and how much they had to lose. It affected me greatly. I can only imagine the effect it had on my black teammates, at whom the slurs were directly targeted. They said they were fine. The hurt, though, must have been enormous.

For the most part, though, we lived in a pocket of calm. We were safe, and our differences were accepted, and ever since, I have believed without question that the single most important priority of government is to provide for the safety of its people. Each and every American is entitled to the same freedoms and, yes, the same sense of security I felt as a kid.

One of my best friends, as a kid and now as an adult, was Dickie Jackson, one of the principals in the Bull Hill shortwave radio fiasco. We spent all our free time together in high school. He succeeded me as mayor of Peekskill, and when I was elected governor I appointed him commissioner of the Department of Motor Vehicles. He's an extremely bright, dedicated, passionate man—a terrific guy—and when we were growing up, it never once occurred to me that he was a different color. Our differences didn't mean anything, and the great thing about Peekskill in the 1950s and early 1960s was that they didn't mean much to most of our neighbors, either.

Dickie even took my cousin Margaret to one of our high school dances, and no one in my family thought twice about it. This was 1963, at the height of the civil rights movement, but to us it was the most natural thing in the world. The people in town who might have had a problem with it didn't seem to care, and the few who did were open-minded enough to assume that Dickie and my cousin knew what they were doing.

We double-dated that night, and I remember my girlfriend's mother, an outspoken working-class woman who had emigrated from Italy, trying to make sense of the arrangement. This woman was not a shrinking violet. She worked in a sewing factory. She stood up for what she believed and said what was on her mind.

"I don't think this is right," she said, "a black boy going with a white girl." There was no enmity in her voice, but she was curious.

"Oh, come on," my cousin said. "What's wrong with it?"

"I just don't think it's right."

"What's not right about it?" I wanted to know. "What difference does it make?"

She couldn't say, but she offered us cookies and lemonade, and we sat around and talked about it. Dickie was made to feel as welcome in her home as we were, and we soon moved on to another line of conversation. That's how it was in Peekskill when I was growing up; everything was right up front and out there and talked about. You could have an honest disagreement with your neighbor, but no one ever said, "You can't come into my home," or, "You can't do this." People were fair and open-minded.

This wide acceptance was a good thing, but we Hungarians still felt a special bond. There was a closeness among the Hungarian community that transcended other relationships.

For a time, the New York Jets were the pride of Hungarian Peekskill. They were our favorite football team, back when they were originally called the Titans in the American Football League, because they trained in Peekskill, at the campus of the Peekskill Military Academy. And then they went out and drafted Joe Namath, a Hungarian, and we hugged them even closer; Namath stood not only as the hope of the AFL but as the hope of each and every Hungarian in town. By our lights, they had always been the Peekskill Jets, but now we could truly lay claim to them.

They were all over Peekskill, all summer long. Namath. Maynard. Snell. Boozer. All of them. We'd climb the fence to watch them play, and look for them on the street on their days off. Sometimes we'd be out in the schoolyard, playing a pickup game of our own, and a couple of the players would stop to watch *us* play. It was just enormously exciting, to have these great pros in our midst, and what was even more exciting was that they were walking around eating our fruit. The players didn't come out to the farm themselves, but the press corps did. They'd buy up all our fruit, just to have it to give out to the players, in the hope of getting a good story out of them. Grandpa made them pay for it all, of course; we couldn't afford to give away our fruit, even to such dignitaries as the New York Jets.

One summer, though, my father had the inspiration to give each player a watermelon with his name carved into the skin. When the watermelons were small, he took a knife and carved out the players' names, and as the watermelons grew the names grew along the outer skins. When training camp broke, the melons were ready, and we carted them down to the field to present them to the players. My father was enormously proud—especially of the chance to show Joe Namath the tremendous fruit we could grow on our little Hungarian farm. The press corps all had their cameras out, anxious for a photo opportunity to break the monotony of the preseason, and as the players stepped up to shake my father's hand and collect their watermelons the shutters clicked away.

Then it was Namath's turn. He took one look at the melon, with the letters N-A-M-U-T-H carved into the skin, and broke into a wide smile. "You call yourself Hungarian?" he said to my father. "You can't even spell my name!" We all laughed. It was a great day.

One of the all-time great rituals from my grandparents' corner of Hungary was the family bacon roast, and it was ours as well. Grandpa made sure of that. Every summer Sunday, when the weather was good, he gathered the family and put out a traditional feast. He'd set an immense slab of bacon on a stick over an open fire, underneath which he'd place a tray of unsliced breads from the local bakery. The tradition was to pile a thick slice of bread high with lettuce, cucumbers, peppers, onions, and radishes. You would then roast the bacon on the fire and let the fat drip onto the bread.

The treat for the adults was a dash of hot pepper on the bread; the treat for the kids was the bacon itself. There was never much left after we'd roasted all the fat out of it, but my father always carved off little pieces as it cooked, just enough so we could get a taste. He made a game out of it. He'd put a slice of bacon in one hand and hold out two fists, and the kids had to line up and guess which hand the bacon was in. One of my cousins figured out that the bacon was hot, and that if he waited long enough my father's hand would start to shake, and that would be the clue, but Dad wasn't one to be outsmarted by a child. He'd look right at my cousin and say, "That's it; you're out," and send him back to the end of the line.

Those wonderful, greasy breads and the dried slices of bacon were the stars of the whole show, but for me the point was mostly the bringing together of friends and family, and the celebration of what we grew on the farm. Everything we ate we grew ourselves—other than the pig and the bread. The grown-ups even drank our own wine, and I later learned you needed the wine to cut the grease and the hot pepper.

It was a wonderful thing, to be so self-sufficient, to have so little and yet so much. Even as a child, I looked on Sundays as the best time of all on the farm; apple-picking time came close, but we were all so busy working then that we never had time to reflect, to visit, to enjoy. Here, each Sunday, we could eat like the pigs the bacon had come from, and then work it off by talking and laughing and walking around the farm, catching up on our lives. Time seemed to stop, and the rest of the world to pause. This was what we worked for, all week long.

As we grew older, and my generation began to scatter, we kept coming back to the farm for Grandpa's bacon roasts. They took place with less frequency, but they remained our link to the farm, and to each other. My daughter Emily remembers the roasts with a fondness that surprises me. Our other children are too young for the ritual to have taken hold, but Emily remembers. She even wrote about it in an essay for her college applications. She wrote about how disgusting it was, with all the fat drippings and the abundance of food, how politically incorrect, how mortified her friends always were to see her family behaving like gluttons. And yet she too looks back on those afternoons as some of the happiest times of her childhood. She loved the feast, but mostly she loved the fact that we were together, marrying the old traditions to our new world.

It is a tradition we still follow each summer, with the new generation of cousins. These relationships cut across economic and social lines. We were rich and poor (or, rather, poor and poorer), but we were all rich with tradition, faith, and dignity. We were Catholics. We went to church. A great many of our friends and neighbors were Jews, Baptists, or Protestants, and they came to church right along with us. Mass on Sunday usually took place without my father, though. He was busy working, and he used to tell us that God would understand. I suspect He did, although my uncle John didn't necessarily share this view. John's family went to church every Sunday and showed up at the farm in the early afternoon, after brunch. This was sometimes a source of tension. John's family would spend an hour at church, and then an hour having brunch, and my father resented having to do all the work by himself. God looks beyond church, he told my uncle, all the time. He looks at how you act and how you live. What counts is being able to look inside yourself and know you're doing the right thing.

Dignity was just as important as faith and tradition, and the Hungarian community was rich in this as well. There was one family that was very close to ours, for many years. They were good people. They were one of the few families in town who thought *we* were prosperous, which gives a good idea how little they had. They lived in a tiny shack, and they were vegetarians, by default. Grandpa let them come to the farm and pick all the vegetables we couldn't sell or use ourselves. He told them they were actually helping him out by carting the stuff away and saving him the cost of the labor. There were six kids in this family, and this was how they survived.

I think back to that poor Hungarian family when I consider the welfare reforms confronting the state, and the nation at large. I think back also to the ways we were all made to live, and work, and the constant struggle to get by, and I weigh these recollections against the way we look on welfare today. For too long, about the only thing our welfare system succeeded at was trapping people in dependency and destroying the family unit.

Many New Yorkers on welfare undoubtedly did a kind of cost-benefit analysis. They're smart. They looked at what was going on. They looked at their options and saw where they might wind up. They saw a short-term solution to a long-term problem, and they grabbed it. They didn't realize the benefit in working hard, and they didn't see the point in paying taxes and giving up benefits like health care, cash allowances, and food stamps if they didn't have to. But the better option, the option we're reconstructing the system to highlight, involves some discipline. We must encourage our children to stay in school, to get a job, to find a way to advance themselves to another level. We should require a person, if able-bodied, to work, to get proper training, to go through workfare. To do this we need to send a message that work is its own reward, and the path not only to a decent future but to a better present.

People are not dumb. Low-income, welfare-dependent people have far more intelligence, ability, and judgment than many in the liberal elite give them credit for, and they're not about to act against their self-interest. They could see they were better off on welfare than taking a minimum-wage job, so they stayed home. According to a study by the Cato Institute, when I took office as governor you could be working full-time, earning more than one and a half times the minimum wage, and still make less than someone on welfare, taking into account related benefits like health care, food stamps, and subsidized housing. The math was absurd, and the people could see that. Of course, they were not going to want to work, under those circumstances. We needed to find a way to show them that it was in their interest to work, and to respect their efforts enough so that their return to the workforce was more worthwhile than staying home and doing nothing.

When I was a kid, we worked because we were supposed to work. We didn't get paid, and naturally there were times when we would have rather been out swimming or playing basketball; but the work needed to get done, we had no choice but to do it, and we were taught to take pride in doing it right. The message was that work, in itself, was valuable—not because you got paid for it, but because of what you could achieve, what you could contribute, what it meant. I can't listen without cringing to a political argument about whether it's humane to make our welfare recipients go back to work. Of course they should work, if they're physically able; to do any less is antithetical to how I was raised and what I believe. I simply can't accept a welfare system that encourages dependency, that tells people that despite their abilities or talents or education it is not their responsibility to work, that it is society's responsibility to take care of them.

When I took office as governor New York's welfare system left millions of New Yorkers feeling isolated and disconnected—from productive society, from their communities, from the economy, from themselves. The economic cost was billions of dollars. The social cost was incalculable.

I suspect that people might read these words and dismiss them as a cliché or a simplistic take on a complex problem. But the consequences of this failed welfare system to us as a people were staggering. Look at the impact in New York of that failed system. In the Peekskill of my youth, there were poor people all around, but there was no underclass. The poor simply had less money, not less talent or ability, and in our world those poor were just as likely to be the next postal workers, the next scholarship recipients, the next mayors, as they were to be the next people in need of government help. I was taught to believe, as Colin Powell so eloquently reminded us, that it is "shameful" to go on welfare unless you are sick or disabled. Not so in New York in 1994. Welfare had become a way of life, and the only shame was that we had allowed the program to deteriorate to that point. It was a seductive, attractive, and ultimately destructive way of life for too many New Yorkers.

Welfare reform—real, fundamental change of a destructive system— was one of my top priorities as governor. It had to be. It is impossible for us to move forward as a people without a sense of common purpose, a common identity, a common belief in a better future. Admittedly, most of us could move forward in a sense, but the wonder of America is that our strength as a nation in significant part depends on the American dream, however we define it individually, burning alive and real for all of us, and that wasn't happening with so many trapped on welfare.

If the failure of the welfare system was obvious, I thought, so too were the solutions. First, responsibility. If you're a parent on welfare, the least you can do is see that your child goes to school, and so we passed Learnfare, which basically provided that if a child had too many unexcused absences from school, the *parent* would lose some of his or her cash benefits. If a teenager found herself pregnant, there would be no more free apartment and no separate package of benefits. She could stay at home and deal with the consequences of her decision without her own check or her own place to live. And if people tried to cheat the system, we installed tough criminal sanctions against fraud, and finger-imaging and computer checks to ensure that only those entitled to benefits actually received them.

Second, work. If you're able, you work. If you couldn't find a job, we would give you Workfare—helping on public projects that wouldn't otherwise get done—in exchange for your benefit check. We would provide the support—child care, job training, assistance with transportation—but you would have to get out there and do the work.

And third, common sense. The system needed to be rational. If you were able to secure a private-sector job at a low salary, we would work a formula to allow you to keep a portion of your payments for a period of time, and your health benefits for a year. Included in this plan would be an opportunity to purchase affordable health care for your children, if your new job didn't offer benefits. We also put a lifetime cap on benefits: five years, to forestall the thinking that welfare was an ongoing lifestyle instead of a program designed to offer temporary relief in a time of need.

The results have been astounding. Without kicking anyone eligible out of the system, or changing eligibility beyond the changes outlined above, we have seen our welfare rolls drop by more than 479,000 people in a little less than three years. Think of it: Nearly a half-million New Yorkers are no longer making the wrong choices for their futures; hundreds of thousands are on the right path—to a better tomorrow and their own piece of the American dream. The right message is finally getting through.

New York had the highest level of dependency in America, and I wasn't about to allow that to continue unchallenged while I was governor. It had to stop. Someone had to push able-bodied people to work, to keep their kids in school, to be responsible citizens. We are on our way, but we are not there yet. I truly don't believe we are remotely close to what we can achieve as a people. There are no real limits. Our lives are certainly far richer than they've ever been, by almost every measure, and there's no reason we can't go far beyond where we are today. I look around and see how we can be inspired by all these new discoveries, from genetic engineering to Internet technology. I see an explosion of belief in a future with no known boundaries.

But we won't get far with a nation divided, with a permanent underclass. We must reach for these changes together, as a people and as a nation.

The Peekskill of my childhood was a working-class, blue-collar community. When we stepped off the team bus for a high school basketball game in an affluent community like Scarsdale, we were all momentarily ashamed of our shabby uniforms, but we held our heads high and we played hard. We Patakis may have been poorer in dollars and cents than many in our poor community, but we had it better than others. And yet I don't recall there being any disgrace in any of our situations. There was no disgrace, even, in the way our poorer friends came to the farm to pick their fill; we were their assistance, until a job or a better situation presented itself. We all might have been on the low end of Peekskill's socioeconomic scale, but we managed. In fact, we did better than that; we worked hard for what little we had; there was dignity in each day, and hope.

The Peekskill of today is somewhat different. When I ran for mayor, and for the assembly, I made it an election eve routine to go door to door through Bohlmann Towers, a high-rise, low-income housing project on Main Street, and I did so because it never ceased to amaze me. My campaign staff always thought I was crazy to give over such an important chunk of such an important night to such an unimportant task, but to me there was nothing more important. There were no Republican votes to be found in Bohlmann Towers, it was said, and this may have been largely true. But there were talented people there. There were bright people, caring people. Some of these Bohlmann residents had tremendous ability, and under different circumstances, under the *right* circumstances, they should have had the opportunity to work, to excel—not just to earn a decent living, but to lead.

What I saw, stepping in and out of those apartments, was the complete opposite of the negativism of the media during the course of a campaign, where the unspoken message is that the public doesn't have a clue, and that our welfare recipients don't want to work. Well, the public does indeed have a clue, and the vast majority of our welfare recipients do indeed want to work; I could see it, going door to door in a building where the police didn't even want to patrol. I could hear it in the voices of these people, and see it in the way they kept their homes; and what I kept thinking, on these visits, was that we have to find a way to get these good people respecting and believing in themselves once more. They don't need the government to do it for them. We need to light a fire under them, to empower them to go out and achieve everything they possibly can. But it's not just lighting a fire; it's removing a chain as well; it's telling them that they will no longer be better off hanging out on a street corner, or sitting at home, than they'll be if they go out and work; it's putting in place a program that will truly benefit all of us, for all time. It's respecting the dignity of work. Yes, there will still be poor people, less able or less motivated than others. But there will be no underclass, no permanent dependence. There will be hope, opportunity, an ability to dream.

6

The Political Life

NATIONAL POLITICS, TO A KID GROWING UP ON A FARM IN Peekskill, New York, meant far less than the National League pennant race, which was important only because that would determine who would take on the beloved Yankees that fall. All of this changed dramatically, however, in October 1956, in a way that is with me still. The Hungarian revolution of 1956 I took in over television, filtered through the collective experiences of my family, and it has stayed with me ever since. Each day was filled with incredible euphoria at the thought of a liberated Hungary, only to be followed by absolute despair at the sight of the Russian tanks running through the streets of Budapest. These were our people, our family. It was as if our own lives were in danger and our own freedom were in jeopardy. What I understood, at eleven, was that our friends and relatives back home were being killed. All they wanted was to be free, and all the Soviets wanted was to deny them that freedom. They wanted to impose their communist, empire-building views on people who clearly rejected them.

I watched the television reports through my grandfather's eyes and worked to understand what they meant. I watched as my father strained to make out the cries and lamentations of the Hungarians underneath the broadcasters' English translation, because he felt that the truth of what was happening was to be found only in the country's native tongue. I didn't speak Hungarian, but I knew certain phrases, enough to recognize the tragedy of the moment and the hopelessness in the voices of the Hungarian people, my extended family. I knew that while we might have been poor by New York standards, we were certainly wealthy in the eyes of our Hungarian relatives. Indeed, one of the great rituals on the farm had been packing and sorting old clothes to send back home, but that all stopped in 1956. There were no more packages, no more letters back and forth. Within the community, these efforts were supplanted by relief drives at Peekskill High School, Drum Hill Junior High School, or the Kossuth Street Church; and the next months saw yet another wave of immigration to our growing city, as Hungarian refugees came to Peekskill to be with family and friends.

I'll never lose those moments—aunts, uncles, cousins, all of us huddled around our small, black-and-white television set, not wanting to hear what the next bulletin had to tell us, but knowing that we couldn't miss a word. The precious link to the lives my grandparents left behind died during that revolution, and there was nothing to do but sit with them and watch, and cry. We were Americans first, proud and patriotic Americans, but there was a piece of each one of us back in Hungary, and those pieces were dying.

Perhaps the most troubling piece in those days of revolution was the up-and-down nature of the reports that made it back to Peekskill. For a time, it appeared the Hungarian freedom fighters would triumph over the Soviets, and there was a stretch of days in there when it seemed all of Peekskill was caught in a shared euphoria over Hungary's prospects. We'd listen for each development in the roller-coaster conflict and celebrate each triumph: The Soviet-controlled soldiers of the Hungarian army did not move to silence the initial uprising of thousands of students in Joszef Bem square, in Budapest, but instead showed solidarity with their friends and neighbors by helping to disarm Russian tanks; they did this by puncturing the reserve-fuel tanks with sharp objects and setting a match to the gasoline, a strategy taught to the Hungarian youths by Russian troops to guard against an invasion from the West. In Budapest, protesters toppled a statue of Joseph Stalin. At Killian Barracks, Hungarian soldiers held off Russian tanks with rocks and bullets and Molotov cocktails. The cumulative message was that the Hungarian spirit and courage were indomitable, but eventually these uplifting reports were replaced with the dispiriting reality that this small country could not possibly do battle with the giant Soviet military machine.

We were all deeply connected to the truths and emotions being played out in our news reports, and there was no looking away. Indeed, these emotions drew me back to Hungary as an adult, in 1995, and on my very first trip to Grandpa's village I was reminded of the revolution. There was no escaping it, even after so many years. I was riding along a small two-lane highway with my wife, Libby, when a county official turned to me and said, in halting English, "This is a very sad road." I asked why, and he told me that this was the road the Russian tanks had come down to go into Budapest. I looked out my window and tried to guess what that moment had been like, but the years had erased the outward signs of that devastation; the oppression was etched on the face of almost everyone I met, but the landscape was back to what it had been.

It wasn't until we actually reached the village that the invasion resonated more intimately. In New York I had met a man who had grown up in Kisvarda, the large town outside my grandparents' small village where my grandfather had lived for a few years, sleeping in churchyards and trying to find opportunity where it didn't exist. As a boy, he had lived across the street from the neighborhood bakery, and he recounted to me how he couldn't cross the street for thirty-six hours during the height of the invasion, because the tanks were coming through so quickly. Finally, one of the Russian drivers fell asleep at the wheel and drove his tank into one of the buildings, stalling the procession. The boy's mother told him to run across the street to the bakery to grab something while he could; the family had nothing to eat, so he crossed the street and bought a few loaves of bread and hurried back, and in the retelling of this ordeal I saw myself. He would have been about the same age as I was when I watched the revolution on television, and he had been in the middle of it—precisely where I might have been if my grandparents had not had the courage and the enterprise to seek a better life in America. He had suffered; and though we suffered too, by extension, it was not the same.

On all my trips to Hungary, I've been reminded of what might have been. The very first time I went to Budapest, when the Iron Curtain was still up, was one of the great disappointments of my life. We planned to stay about a week, but I barely made it through one night. There was a despotic air about the place, a sense of resignation. There was no joy in the eyes of the people, and very little hope.

We took the train from Vienna, and when we reached the Hungarian border we could see that it was rimmed with miles and miles of barbed-wire fencing illuminated by searchlights on watchtowers. It was like something from a bad cold war movie of the 1950s, except that it was real, in the 1970s. The guards stopped the train, and boarded, and then the most amazing thing happened. One of the border guards approached, a young man no older than twenty, and he had Pataki written all over him; in fact, he looked exactly like my cousin Bobby. He was six foot four, with big square shoulders and a square jaw, and I thought to myself, He's got to be a cousin. The resemblance was uncanny. My heart lifted, but then it sank when I realized what this young man was about to do. I was afraid to talk to him—not for what he might say, but for how he might sound. I sat there in this cold, despairing place and tried to find some comfort in this strange bond, but it wouldn't come. Yes, this border guard looked just like Bobby, and in my romantic view, we could have been distant relatives, but it was his job to search me and my belongings and all the other Americans on that train.

The border guards were looking for contraband—specifically, for radios. In Hungary, all radios were sold without tuners (they were preset to sanctioned stations), but the government couldn't control the airwaves; you could pick up a cheap transistor radio in Vienna and tune in to Radio Free Europe, or any other broadcast with a strong enough signal, so the Soviets went to great lengths to keep any outside radios from infiltrating the border.

It was such a depressing experience, to be searched at the gateway to my grandparents' homeland by a young man with my cousin's face. Once we got to Budapest, it was even more disheartening. Outside the train station, we had to run the black market gauntlet, racing past dozens of men and women eager to rent us a car or a room, or to sell us a meal; the atmosphere was seedy and treacherous, and not at all what we were expecting. We couldn't check our bags through to the hotel, because they needed to be searched again. Everyone looked so fearful, so mistrustful. We walked down the hills to the Danube, and people wouldn't look at us because we were wearing decent clothes and it was clear we didn't belong.

My disappointment was compounded by the special bond I had felt with my grandparents' country. I'd heard so many wonderful things about Budapest—that it was the Paris of the communist bloc; that it was enchanting and sophisticated—and I'd been very much looking forward to my first visit, but the entire city struck me as cheerless. The weather was horrible, too. It was pouring when we pulled up to the hotel, and we drove past a line of Mercedes limousines waiting to collect a group of Russian generals assembled under a canopy, and just off to the side were their Hungarian drivers, standing in the rain. It was such a hypocritical scene, and I ached for the way the people of Hungary were made to conduct themselves. I took it personally. I decided right then that I couldn't stay another night. Any longer and I'd probably have been arrested, or shot, because I couldn't sit back as a free man, as an American whose family came from Hungary, and accept the Soviets' treatment of these people.

The next morning, when Libby and I presented the border guards with our papers, they detained us for what seemed an unusually long time. They could see I had a Hungarian name, and that I'd arrived only the night before, and they were suspicious. They did another thorough search, after which they asked why we were leaving so soon.

"Because I can't stand the Russian soldiers," I said, in my best Hungarian. Of course, this didn't exactly endear me to the guards; it made them even more suspicious, and they did another search. This troubled me, but only a little. We were taking out a wonderful bottle of Tokaj wine, from my grandfather's region.

This wine was special—so special that I had no qualms about having it, even though it wasn't supposed to be exported. The ban made no sense in my worldview, and at that time in my life I wasn't conditioned to respond to the arbitrary mandates of oppression. I figured that the worst they could do was confiscate the bottle. It was a chance worth taking, and to better my chances I assisted in the deception. Each time, when a guard asked me to point out my bags, I indicated two of our three suitcases. They searched those two bags right down to the seams, but it never occurred to them that we had another, and so the bag with the wine remained untouched, despite their exhaustive scrutiny. Nothing happened, and we made off with the wine, and the entire episode struck me as about what you can expect from totalitarianism. It's rigid, unbending, and unthinking, and it doesn't work.

Back in 1956, in Peekskill, the Hungarian Revolution had left me thinking for the first time about the way our own government worked, about the qualities of our freedom, about American politics. I was only eleven, but we talked about these things on the farm. Until 1956, I'd taken freedom for granted. (Even my grandparents, in some ways, had grown so comfortable with their freedom that they expected nothing less.) Government stood for us as a benevolent force. It could build a road or fix a park or offer relief to those in need. It could help us honor our heroes and censure our villains. And then, from out of nowhere, I saw these powerful images on television, showing the tremendous power of the wrong kind of government to crush people's spirits and take not just their freedom, but even their lives.

Underneath these images, I wondered if Hungary could ever get to where we were, or if America itself would fall to the Soviets. Remember that falling to the Soviets wasn't beyond reason to a small boy during the middle 1950s—the threat of communism was all around; you couldn't switch on the television or open a newspaper without seeing Senator McCarthy on one of his crusades against the "red menace." It was a time of relative peace, but the talk was about bomb shelters, air raid drills in our public schools, and global tension. To an eleven-year-old boy, who absorbed the atrocities in Hungary as if they were happening to his own family, anything was possible, and this was never more apparent than during the 1956 Olympic Games, in Melbourne, Australia. It is the tradition, in Olympic villages, to fly the Olympic flag, the Greek flag, and the flag of the host nation, but for the 1956 games the Australians raised the Hungarian flag instead of their own. I looked on and felt a tremendous rush of pride at such a bold show of support for my grandparents' homeland. I took it personally, and it meant the world. It meant even more when Hungary's gold-medal water-polo team faced off against the Russians and shut them out, 4–0. It was such a violent, hotly contested match that by the end of it the pool was filled with blood—literally; the Hungarian team was playing not only to win, but to get back at their opponents and what they stood for.

So, yes, anything was possible—even the blood sport of politics, played out on the world stage, in no less an arena than the Olympic Games.

The other memorable anticommunist event that touched Peekskill occurred when I was four years old, and obviously too young to remember it firsthand. When it was all over, Peekskill ended up making national headlines, although it was never entirely clear how the news reflected on our community, only that it did.

It was the summer of 1949, and Paul Robeson was scheduled to give a concert on a farm just outside of town. Robeson was a wonderful, deep-throated singer, perhaps at the height of his popularity; but he was also an avowed communist, and the concert was largely perceived as a left-wing political rally. He had staged a similar concert in nearby Mohegan Colony the previous summer, and it had turned into a platform for the singer's leftist views. In fact, the 1949 "concert" was scheduled in Peekskill only after it had been determined the Mohegan Colony couldn't hold the anticipated crowd, which newspaper accounts would later put at about 15,000—an enormous figure in a working-class community that numbered about the same.

The idea of hosting a communist rally was anathema to my parents and grandparents, and to their friends. My grandparents had come to this country, early in the century, to avoid the kind of government intrusion represented by Robeson's views. And by all accounts, the transplant had taken: They were, some forty years later, genuinely patriotic and grateful for the opportunities this country had provided for their families, for people who had come with nothing. They were proud to be Americans (and Democrats), and they were mindful of any movement or uprising that might threaten their adopted homeland. To be sure, it was perfectly legal for a communist group to meet and organize, but to place it in context, the rally was shortly before the McCarthy hearings and the "red scare" that would grip the entire nation, and shortly after Winston Churchill had traveled to Independence, Missouri, to declare in a much-heralded address that the next great threat to world peace would come from behind the Iron Curtain. The emerging notion of communism, just after the war, played very much into the fear of many immigrants that the freedoms they now enjoyed were suddenly endangered. One of those freedoms, of course, was the freedom of speech, and the right to gather and exchange ideas in a public forum.

This, I came to believe, was what led to the events of that summer. A number of our Peekskill neighbors, sparked by the local American Legion and other veterans in the area, gathered to protest the Robeson rally. My father wasn't a veteran; the poor eyesight that he had inherited from his mother (and that I inherited from him) made military service impossible under all but the most catastrophic circumstances. But many of his friends from the post office had served, and together they went out to the concert site with their picket signs, expecting to

My grandfather John Pataki and my father, Louis.

Grandpa Pataki and me (at age four), pitching hay for the haystacks.

The famous tented tomato plants.

That's my father directing the firefighters (at the right).

Dad in the Peekskill post office, around 1960.

My mother at Depew Park in Peekskill, 1936.

Me with Mom, my maternal grandfather, Matteo Lagana, and my older brother, Lou, at the boatyard.

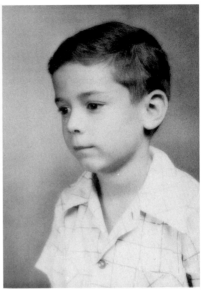

A more demure me, a few years later.

Big Chief George Pataki, age two.

This is about as far as my football career went.

My big brother, Lou, and me on one of those great summer days. Note the grapevines in the back.

Grandpa Pataki making Hungarian wine.

Me (second from the top), Lou (behind me), and cousins galore in the haystack . . .

. . . and bundled up for sledding (I'm front and center, wearing the big scarf).

Happy ham radio operators at work.

Graduation Day at Yale . . .

. . . and Wedding Day, July 14, 1973.

We visited Libby's parents while on our honeymoon!

Libby.

Family life is the best there is.

Emily visits me in the
Senate Chamber,
1993.

Mementos of the
campaign trail.

A governor's perk—riding with Joe
DiMaggio.

Victory Night, 1994—
Hungarian style.

Howard Stern, my
self-appointed campaign
manager.

On the job . . . and off
duty.

stand up for what they believed. There were nearly 1,000 veterans and their supporters lined up in protest, because just as Robeson had a right to sing and speak his mind, so too did patriotic Americans like my father have the right to protest his appearance, as long they weren't disruptive. We still have the picket sign my father carried that night—"Wake up, America"—and for years I would get a glimpse of the phrase, lit through the dust-beams in our attic, without fully understanding the message behind it or the events underneath it.

My mother listened on the radio (she was home with us kids), and the story of what happened quickly passed into family lore. What was to have been a peaceful protest turned into a riot. A man was killed. Eight people were hospitalized. A hundred others suffered minor injuries. Cars were overturned and windows broken. The concert stage was smashed, and sheet music was burned. *Time* magazine called the "sorry" affair "an example of misguided patriotism and senseless hooliganism, more useful to communist propaganda than a dozen uninterrupted song recitals by Paul Robeson." The event's organizers had secured the proper permits, and there was an ample security force, but the protesters still had their way. The rally was canceled. And my mother was stuck at home with her two small children, listening on the radio to what was happening, thinking that her husband was out there, leading an angry mob, or—worse—being beaten by an angry mob turned in on itself.

Thankfully, my father wasn't hurt in the melee, and in fact had left for home before the protest ever erupted into violence, but that didn't diminish his role. He respected the law, but he knew the men who helped to make the protest ugly. I grew up knowing these men as well, and to me the most troubling aspect is that I'm not sure how I would have responded.

When I was old enough to understand, I deplored the way the event reflected our community. While I loved that Peekskill stood as a symbol of anticommunism, I disliked the fact that Paul Robeson had been denied a forum for his views, however distasteful and anti-American those views might have been. I was shocked that the police had looked away and that people had been hurt. Mostly, I disliked that what had been clearly a pro-American, anticommunist protest had been portrayed across the nation as a racist, antiblack, and anti-Semitic rally that introduced the city of Peekskill to millions of Americans. I still meet people all across the country whose only knowledge of Peekskill came from the headlines in their local newspapers the following morning, almost fifty years ago. I was saddened by the fact that, when given the chance, we didn't show ourselves to best advantage.

One of the ironic footnotes to the riot is the friendship I now enjoy with Pete Seeger, the legendary folk musician. He lives upstate in Beacon, about ten miles north, and he was a vibrant presence on the music scene in those days. He also demonstrated some leftist leanings of his own, which was certainly his right, and he was loudly critical of the community for shutting down the concert. He wasn't scheduled to perform at the Robeson concert himself, but he supported it just the same.

Afterward, Seeger vowed never to perform in Peekskill, a promise he kept for more than thirty years, until I became mayor. I respected his position but hoped he might reconsider. We had just renovated the historic Paramount Theater downtown, and I invited Seeger and his Clearwater Singers to play there. He had been active in several environmental causes throughout his career, and he saw that we were doing some positive things with the riverfront area, and he decided it no longer made sense to hold against the town the unfortunate events of so long ago.

So Pete Seeger came to Peekskill and played, and it was wonderful. We've since seen each other on several occasions, but I've never told him that my father was out there picketing on the night of the riot, to stand and be counted, to rail against a movement that was plainly un-American. But I also understand the full spectrum of emotions that followed the event, and I let Pete sing in Peekskill in peace.

Around this time I was introduced to a bona-fide member of the federal government—Congressman Ralph Gwynn—and our meeting was probably the closest I came to a genuine lightbulb-over-the-head revelation of what I wanted to do when I grew up. I was about twelve or thirteen, and in the back of my head I always thought I'd be a farmer; but somewhere closer to the front I imagined I'd find a way to mix farming with a life of the mind. I certainly never thought of politics as any kind of career. I had met the mayor, and some of the local leaders, but Congressman Gwynn was the first politician I'd met who actually worked in Washington. (Goodness, he probably even knew the president!) All of a sudden, I became terribly excited about how Washington worked, and how one man could help make a difference.

Throughout most of my growing up, Ralph Gwynn represented the Hudson Valley, which of course included Peekskill. Our meeting was arranged by a man named Ray Lapolla, a close friend of my parents. I was friendly with his son, Fran. Ray Lapolla's full-time job was as the sports editor of the local newspaper, but he also helped out in the congressman's Peekskill office. One night, he and his son took me and my mother up to the Gwynns' farm in Pawling, for dinner. I no longer recall how the evening came about, but I am grateful that it did. I was instantly infatuated with the congressman's job—and with the congressman himself. He spoke passionately and intelligently about world issues, and yet he still lived and worked on the family farm. He was a regular person, living a regular life, and yet somehow in the midst of extraordinary issues and events. What a great setup, I thought—to be able to work in Washington and help change people's lives without materially changing your own! The congressman continued as a farmer (in many ways, he said, farming remained a priority), but he went down to Washington when Congress was in session, reflecting the views of his district, expressing his own beliefs, and coming back to continue the dialogue at home. All this fostered in me an idealistic view of government and democracy—a view I still hold, because I see no reason to be anything less than idealistic when it comes to making our government function at its best.

I remember thinking how great it could be if all our congressmen had another job to go home to at night. As a kid, this was what I thought about. It's what I still think about. I believe all elected officials should be more like Ralph Gwynn; we should all have something, a family business, profession, trade, or career to ground us as leaders, something to go back to when our time in office runs out or our ideas fall from favor. I loved the idea that this important man, this congressman, had another life, another career outside politics. The more I've seen of government, the more important it seems to me that our leaders have outside interests and not just seek a permanent government career. This is why I believe term limits are vital to the long-range health of this nation, at every level of government. We should get in, have our say, and get out. I can't stress this position enough, even though it runs counter to the viability of most political careers—including my own. We should vote our conscience, as elected officials, and enact legislation because we think it's the right thing to do, not because it's what we think we need to do to get reelected.

Throughout my first term as governor, I was constantly being asked if I planned to run for reelection in 1998; I suspected I would, but I was never entirely sure. And yet the media types who covered my administration didn't understand that I was not obsessing about 1998. They have no frame of reference for that type of thinking. What I planned to do, I told them, is everything I could to make New York a better state, on the assumption that I'm *not* going to be around for another four years. I like to think there's a lot more good we could do if I *am* going to be around; but if I'm not, there would be a lot of pluses to that as well. I'd be able to spend more time with my family. I'd have occasional weekends and fall afternoons off. I'd be out from under the intense public scrutiny and second-guessing. My time, once again, would be my own and my family's.

The possibility of losing, or walking away, doesn't bother me nearly as much as the idea of overstaying my welcome. This, to me, is the only way to approach a career in politics without losing sight of what drew you to public service in the first place. To people for whom politics is all there is, a term limit poses a real threat; they're terrified of it. But to someone for whom politics is simply part of a balanced life, a point of pause in a varied career, term limits are only natural. Seeing Ralph Gwynn on his farm that night really crystallized this for me. I loved the idea of being involved in the world and making a difference, and yet still being home. I'd always thought of myself as an ordinary person, living on a farm, working with my hands; and to be able to marry that lifestyle to a political calling was a phenomenal idea. I filed it away for a time I might need it.

My next great political dawning was in 1960, on election day, long past my bedtime. I was fifteen. I stayed up all night, rooting for John F. Kennedy. I loved JFK. He was young, passionate, and inspirational. He was Catholic. He was anticommunist. His vibrant love of country was what struck me the most, as the cold war still raged. We were, by this time, a largely Democratic household, but none of us looked at Kennedy along party lines. We were charmed by his patriotism, his youth, his work ethic, and his religious beliefs, much of which seemed to mirror our own.

I should mention here that our Democratic leanings didn't always translate into votes. My grandmothers didn't vote. My grandfather on the farm didn't drive anything but his horse and wagon, which he couldn't take all the way into town to the polls, so the local party officials sent someone to pick him up to make sure he voted early. That was the Democratic machine back then, working very effectively. My Italian grandfather made a point of voting on his own, and he was for Kennedy. Most of my aunts and uncles and cousins were Democrats. It was, in many ways, a family compound built on a shared ideology, by people who were still a little surprised at their right to vote.

My father, by 1960, was beginning to lean in another direction. He voted for Kennedy, but he started to talk about how the party wasn't strong enough, or varied enough, to deal with our mounting domestic problems. I remember listening to him talk to Ray Lapolla, who had become Congressman Gwynn's campaign manager, and their conversation was all about how the Democratic Party was not strong enough in the fight against communism.

But I was very much a Kennedy supporter. I didn't look beyond what he stood for, as a symbol, but I was charmed by that symbol. More than any other leader of that generation, Kennedy seemed to elevate politics. He transcended politics, in a way. With Kennedy, it wasn't just a matter of the art of governing. It went beyond the presidency. It was a kind of royalty. It was holding a light to an image of America at its best and sharing that image with the rest of the world.

I don't mean to give the impression that government was suddenly all I thought about, because that was hardly the case. If I thought about it at all, I thought about JFK and what he stood for, and I thought about beating back the Russians, but I had other things on my mind. I was still more concerned with basketball, track, science, ham radios, and the farm. I attended an apolitical high school: None of my friends were much interested in government; most of them would not have known what was going on in our own City Hall, unless their fathers or friends of their families were involved.

It wasn't really until I got to Yale, in 1963, where all around me people exchanged ideas as freely as they shook hands, that I was truly bitten by the political bug. Yale itself was an awakening. I wasn't the most worldly kid on the campus, and the first thing that struck me was the traffic. Yale is in a busy downtown area of a large city, New Haven, Connecticut, and I wasn't used to all that noise, all the time. I'd been to New York City, but I'd never lived in New York City. On the farm, in the evenings, there were crickets, and there was the rustling of the wind, but in New Haven there were sirens and buses and the consuming sounds of haste and congestion. It was a major adjustment.

Another big adjustment was class. We may have been poor by Peekskill standards, but we were downright needy on the distorted scale of an elite Ivy League institution like Yale. It was a startling contrast, but fortunately I was so naive that I didn't see it. I'd meet someone named Du Pont and think, Gee, what a funny-sounding name. It never dawned on me that people could actually have that kind of money or own those kinds of companies. In a way, my ignorance was bliss, because I was utterly unintimidated by the social trappings of wealth and power. I didn't even know that such wealth or power existed.

On the other hand, ignorance was no help in the classroom. The academics at Yale took some getting used to. I'd graduated number two in my class in high school, but I was unprepared for this college. At least that's how I felt. People were assuming things I'd never heard of, right off the bat. It really was a bit of a shock, and it took me awhile to feel comfortable and get the lay of the land. There are some people who burst onto the scene and right away you think, Well, this person has presence. That wasn't me. I was the one holding back, checking things out, hoping to get by undetected until I could figure out what was expected of me, what I could expect of myself.

One of the first ways I thought to challenge myself was extracurricular. I still played basketball, but I wasn't good enough to make the varsity, so I funneled my energies into what I thought was the next best thing. I joined the political union, because my brother had joined the political union. Most of what I did in my first months at Yale had to do with what Lou had done. His experience was my guide. Indeed, his experience was why I was there in the first place.

In the beginning I looked on my involvement in the political union as an interesting diversion that was a bit like team sports. That's really all it was for me. Instead of being on the other side of a basketball court, you were on the liberal side or the conservative side of a debate topic. It was us against them, in the same way that a football game was us against them. The political union was tremendous fun and fiercely competitive, and it offered a terrific opportunity to meet new people. Most of all, it opened a window to a whole new way of looking at the world. Before long, it even had me looking differently at President Kennedy. It made me aware that I was more conservative than most Democrats and much more in favor of a limited government. By the fall of 1963, I was no longer a big fan of JFK's policies, even though I still responded to his personality. He was still an inspirational, positive force on the American scene, but he spoke to something different in me. He stood, at the time of his death, as the kind of figure with whom you did not have to agree to admire—much like Ronald Reagan for future generations.

I'll never forget how I heard about Kennedy's assassination in Dallas. It was my freshman year. I was in a calculus class, looking forward to my first Harvard–Yale football game, which was to be held in New

Haven that weekend. The game was, and remains, one of the great rivalries in college sports. There were banners all over Yale, and a tremendous excitement was in the air. The professor was handing back our midterm exams, and I'd gotten 100 percent. I was trying to keep quiet about it, since it wasn't in me to brag or to worry how everyone else had done on the test. I didn't know anything was going on. I'd just come from another class. Then I started to hear all this whispering, and I looked around and saw a lot of people crying, and my first thought was, My, they must have done really lousy on the test. But then the whispering reached me and I was crying too.

I was crushed. The whole campus was thrown into mourning. The football game was canceled. We walked around in a daze for a few days. It struck different people differently, though. One of my roommates, a very left wing guy I'd known only a couple of months, actually argued that Kennedy's death was a good thing, and it was baffling to me that someone could see the assassination in this way. And this was a leftist—this wasn't one of the conservatives from the political union who happened not to like Kennedy. I should have said something to him, but I didn't. I didn't know where to start. I couldn't think clearly. I didn't want to know what it all meant; I wanted only to consider that it had happened.

In an instant, all the joy was drained from politics. The competitive aspect of our debates, the sport . . . all of it was gone. For me, in just these first few weeks away at school, I'd come to see our political combat as somewhat harmless. The free exchange of ideas was an intellectual combat of words, but it was mostly benign. And then, with an assassin's bullet, it was a combat of a different kind. Politics didn't have the same meaning. It was as if we'd been in a boxing ring, where there were rules and the rules were applied, and then the rules were tossed out and it was a jungle and people died and the country suffered. It was an awful time, and to have to listen to my leftist roommate attempt to philosophize about a national tragedy was almost obscene. It was a moment that begged for compassion and humanity, not for political debate.

It's become hackneyed to say that JFK's death changed my generation's view of America; but for someone who experienced it as I did—
at just that time in our history, at just that place, at just my age—it was
a profoundly personal thing. There was an overwhelming loss of innocence, a change from holding a shining light up to the world to setting
loose a dreadful career politician, Lyndon Johnson, who to me represented much that was wrong with our system of government. What
had been a simple time of inexhaustible hope was immediately replaced with backroom dealmaking. Whereas it had been all of us together, it was now, What's in it for me? With Kennedy, we seemed to
take a giant step forward on the world stage, and we were now being
asked to accept two giant steps back. It was possible to believe that
things would never be right again.

It took us all a long time to recover. It truly was as if a light had
gone out. You could argue, as many have argued, that we're just now
getting over the assassination. In between, the heart of this nation has
had to withstand the Vietnam War and Watergate. It took resolutely
positive developments on the world stage, like Ronald Reagan's administration and then the Persian Gulf War, and thirty years of perspective to restore the hope and possibility that I knew as a college
freshman.

In time, the life returned to our political debates at Yale, and I
started to hit my stride as a student. In one class, History 35, Professor
John Morton Blum held forth on the history of twentieth-century
American politics, and I was again transfixed. Professor Blum was the
first person I heard speak about the concept of an activist government;
he'd written a book on Teddy Roosevelt, in which he weighed Roosevelt's activist approach against both a laissez-faire Republican view
and a big-government Wilsonian model. I came away with a lifelong
attachment to Teddy Roosevelt, and an unshakable concept of the
role of an active but limited government in our society. I looked at
Roosevelt—who'd seen an antitrust system that seemed patently unfair, who had broken up the monopolies and created a fair market
structure governed by competition in the private sector—and I recog-

nized that the role of our elected officials was to referee and not to quarterback. Professor Blum's class instilled in me the notion that government should work to change the rules, to create a level playing field, but it should not drive the ball or dictate the course of action.

I returned to the political union with renewed enthusiasm. There's an interesting sidebar to my political experiences here. We had all kinds of people come to campus to speak, and one year we had a number of United States senators address our group. It was always exciting when we could get someone from Washington to come to the campus; it gave us a sense that we were plugged into the workings of the nation. I suppose, in a way, we were.

After these talks, a group of us would usually retire to Mory's, the legendary New Haven drinking establishment just off campus (and home of the Whiffenpoofs), to have a few beers and reflect on what we'd just heard. One night, as sometimes happened, our speaker asked if he might join us. This senator was a wizened old character, with hair dyed orange and a thick southern accent; he was stuck in town for the evening and wanted to go out. He seemed like fun, so we invited him along, thinking there were worse ways to spend an evening.

Mory's was about ten blocks from the political union hall, and the senator announced that he was going to run the whole way. Sure enough, he did—and at a pretty decent pace. It was all we could do to stay with him. A few of us were huffing and puffing by the time we got there, but the senator looked unruffled. He hadn't even broken into a sweat, and once we got inside he proceeded to drink us under the table. The man was nearly seventy, and he outdebated us, outran us, and outdrank us.

The man was Strom Thurmond, the senior senator from South Carolina, and he was a senior citizen even then, in the mid-1960s. I don't agree with everything he's stood for over the years, but I have to admire his grit. In 1996, thirty years after our drinking session at Mory's, he was elected to another six-year term, which would make him over 100 years old before the next election.

When we parted company that night at Mory's, the talk among our group was all about the feisty old senator from South Carolina, and the ways in which our system tended to favor those already in political power. It made some of us think how we might someday go into those corridors of power ourselves. By junior year, I had myself thinking that if I really hit it big and caught every break in the book I might someday be a congressman. I was alone in this. A bunch of us Hudson Valley Conservatives hung out together at Yale, and we used to sit around down at Mory's and assess our peers. We'd think, Oh, he'll be a congressman, and that guy will be a congressman, but nobody ever thought I'd be a congressman. They didn't think I would get that far. Personally, I thought I'd make a great congressman, but I wasn't confident enough to share my assessment with the others.

Even in our private moments, none of us from the Hudson Valley ever dared think of himself as a senator or a governor. That was for the prep school guys, people like John Kerry, who chaired the Liberal Party on campus the semester before I was elected chairman of the Conservative Party. The John Kerrys or the George W. Bushes were the ones who'd one day be running for national office. Jay Harvey Wilkinson III, from Virginia, was the president of the political union, and we all thought he would someday be president of the United States. (He's now a United States judge, and he appears regularly on the short lists for nomination to the Supreme Court, whenever there is a Republican in the White House.)

Me? I was a spear-carrier. I knew my place. I knew that if I did well at Yale, got into a good law school, worked hard, and got lucky, I could end up in Congress, if my interest in government lasted.

I don't know if it was the way I was raised, or some genetic aspect of character, but I've always felt an obligation to do more than simply provide for myself and my family. Providing for a family is important, but I wanted something else—something I enjoyed, something that offered me personal fulfillment and helped us advance as a society. It didn't have to be politics. It could have been medicine. It could have been working for the environment in an area like forest management. I

could have gone into farming and developed new methods of growing grain. I could have gone into business if I saw a way to manu-
facture something new, or to build affordable houses—and have a
positive impact on some community.

One of my goals at that time was to teach, perhaps at the college
level, but I never got around to acting on it. I had become a history
buff, and the idea of teaching fit neatly into my notion of giving something back; and though I never actually applied for a graduate program in history, I thought about it long and hard. I still do, from time
to time, and still hope the opportunity might arise down the road.

Vacations at home allowed me to see a different kind of politics at
the Fleischmann's yeast factory, where I often worked outside the
rules negotiated by Local 42 of the yeastmakers' union, or Local 342 of
the International Brotherhood of Firemen and Oilers. I loved working
at Fleischmann's. It struck me as just the opposite of Marx's sense of
alienation, and a perfect counterweight for an Ivy League student. At
the end of the day, instead of taking notes, writing papers, and going
to classes, I had made yeast or vodka. There would be cases of something I had worked to create being loaded onto a truck or railcar. This
was also why I loved going back to the farm on weekends when we
picked. It was a tangible, fascinating thing (as opposed to an elusive,
fascinating thing), and I absolutely thrilled to it, though Fleischmann's
was grueling, backbreaking work.

It was dangerous, too, and patently unfair to us part-timers. If you
were in the union (which I wasn't, at first), it meant you had to carry
only up to sixty-pound sacks, but if you weren't in the union they'd
take you aside and load you up with two hundred-pound sacks, one
on each shoulder, and send you off to do the work of three union men.
If you were working in the refrigerator, in the yeast building, the
union rule was thirty minutes in the cooler and fifteen minutes out. If
you weren't in the union, they'd leave you in there as long as there
was work to be done. Once, they left me in the cooler for seven hours.
Seven hours! Management didn't care because they knew I couldn't
file a grievance, and the union labor pool didn't care because I wasn't
a member of the local.

They'd leave us in these coolers, or sitting around open vats of formaldehyde, pickling our lungs, making sure the yeast didn't ferment. I thought that if I hyperventilated, I could hold my breath in the time it took to dump the formaldehyde on the yeast to slow the fermenting process. I didn't always make it, but I was successful enough to go back to work the next day and try again. God knows what my lungs look like from breathing in all those chemicals. One breath at the wrong time could literally knock you to the floor.

Local 42 was an extremely tight union, and it rarely made room for us college kids; we were generally laid off whenever we approached the number of days on the job to qualify. The powerhouse, though, was represented by Local 342, and I was eventually invited to join the International Brotherhood of Firemen and Oilers. I still have my union card, although the local has long been defunct. I wanted so badly to get in there, principally because then Fleischmann's couldn't lay me off or take advantage of me the way it took advantage of the yeast-makers. The powerhouse itself, though, was like something out of Dickens. This was the operation that powered the entire plant, and they had us using the same equipment my grandfather had used after his stint at the hat factory. I'd come back to the farm and sit on the porch with him after dinner and talk about the winch we'd use to pull the coal cars, and he'd say, "Yeah, we had the same winch."

I loved the way the job connected me to my grandfather, to my uncle (who had also worked there for a time), and to the first wave of Hungarian immigrants in Peekskill. We're connected still. As I write this, my daughter Emily is working in the same building, as a waitress. A friend of mine recently converted the gin building of the abandoned Fleischmann's factory into a restaurant, and Emily wants to put away a little spending money for college. About the last thing she was thinking of was to continue the line of Patakis toiling in that building into the fourth generation, but it's difficult to run from your legacy in a small town like Peekskill, and foolish to try.

The hardest job I've ever had was working on the coal cars at the Fleischmann's factory, which I did during my second summer home from school. Time had stood still down there. There was an internal train of three or four coal cars, intended to haul about 170 tons of coal. The first would be lined up over a hopper, so that we could open the bottom of the coal car and let the coal fall to an underground crusher; then we'd pull the train up so the next car in line could make the same delivery. The crusher was in a giant pit, beneath the railroad tracks, and from there the coal would travel in wrought-iron buckets in a coal elevator to the sixth floor of the factory, where it would be gravity-fed to the boilers that generated the power for the entire facility.

It was an impressive operation, or at least it must have been when it was first conceived, at the turn of the century. By the time I arrived on the scene, however, the equipment was so old that none of it worked. We had to pry open the bottoms of the coal cars because they were all rusted shut. We had to get into the cars ourselves and use long iron pikes to poke the coal through the slats or shovel it out by hand, because it no longer fell freely; and once in a while we'd fall through the car, past the railroad tracks, and down to the crusher below. Sometimes we could catch ourselves on one of the railroad tracks, but not always. Generally, there was enough coal in the crusher to keep us from getting crushed; we could stand on the coal and pull ourselves out before it was all processed. We were frequently sent down into the crusher by design instead of by accident. The pit was falling apart and leaking, and every half hour or so one of us would have to go down a tiny opening on a little metal ladder and fill some of the buckets by hand.

I used to go through an entire bottle of salt tablets during the course of an eight-hour day. On ninety-degree summer days, I'd sweat like a horse. Union rules said we had to wear a mask down in the pit, but after about a minute it would be soaked through with sweat; I'd wear it on my head, because I was afraid to be caught without it. I'd be down there in the dark, gasping for air, shoveling coal into these buckets, worrying about the work rules.

Some of the work rules made sense. This was the only job I ever had where I was given a half hour of paid time to shower. We came out of those pits totally black; coal dust was in our clothes, in our hair, in our nostrils, in our lungs. A half hour wasn't nearly enough time to scrub out the filth of the day, but it gave us a jump-start on our showers at home. All summer long, I walked around looking as if I'd been caught in an explosion of coal dust. You could always tell the men who worked the cars, because we looked like raccoons; we couldn't rub our eyes hard enough to get the coal dust off.

It was a terrible job, but I put up with it because I was in the union, and because it paid about twenty-five cents more an hour than a shift in the yeast building. It was the best-paying job around, and I discovered that you can put up with a lot when you're young, strong, and unafraid. I discovered also that I have enormous respect for people who work in production and manufacturing. So we have difficulty with the notion of organized labor, but I learned in my time at the Fleischmann's factory that there has to be a balance. Labor unions can be corrupt or unjust, but I choose to believe that fairness will win out in most instances. The work rules in the yeast building and the powerhouse weren't what they should have been, and the interests of the union leaders often ran counter to the interests of management; but if workers do not have the ability to protect themselves there are going to be plenty of employers lined up to exploit them—even to the point where their lives are in danger. One worker in the powerhouse was crushed and killed just months before I started there. It's a question of balance. You don't want government running the show, but you can't allow sleazy employers to kill workers or expose them to unsafe working conditions. For every ninety-nine employers willing to do whatever is appropriate for the workers' safety, there will be one looking for a quick profit at the expense of the people on the line. On the other hand, for unions to unfairly use worker dues to advance their leaders' own national political agenda at the expense of the workers' own interest, as the AFL–CIO did in the 1996 elections, is just wrong.

Daniel Webster once said: "Liberty exists in proportion to wholesome restraint." This is one of my favorite quotations, and I think the sentiment applies here. We need enlightened employers who understand that the employees are part of a team, that they have an obligation to protect workers and an interest in helping them succeed. Some business leaders have come to this position on their own; others have been dragged to it reluctantly; and still others are determined to work their labor pool into the ground. But management must nurture its workers and see that they succeed as the company succeeds. There's no other way, and labor must have the ability to organize or risk being exploited by unenlightened employers. Sometimes the balance tips too far one way, and sometimes it tips too far the other way, but there's nothing inherently wrong with the system. It took being on the short end of it to make me recognize the possibilities.

COLUMBIA LAW SCHOOL WAS ANOTHER KIND OF DAWNING. The world had changed since I had gone off to Yale as an undergraduate. New Haven in 1963 had certainly been a bustling city, but it was also very much a college town; things moved to fairly conventional rhythms. That was an innocent time, on a campus rich in tradition. Throughout my four years there, we had to wear a coat and tie to meals. Drug use may have been on the rise, but it was still almost invisible and very much the exception. People were there to learn, to exchange ideas, and to make their families proud. And their families were from all over; for every New Yorker I met on campus, there was someone from Kansas or South Dakota, someone who couldn't match even the innocent experiences of my childhood in Peekskill.

Columbia in the fall of 1967 had a much more sophisticated, even radical urban flavor. People dressed however they wanted and acted on every impulse. They went to classes when they felt like it or not at all. Drug use was so widespread that it was the norm. The campus was distinctly part of New York; it throbbed with the beat of the inner city—it was near the edge of Harlem—and it was probably the most exciting, tumultuous university environment in the country. The student newspaper, the *Spectator*, actually endorsed Eldridge Cleaver, the radical Black Panther candidate, for president in 1968, which gives an idea of the dominant mind-set. In fact, Columbia was such a radical place that when a few of my most conservative friends supported Hubert Humphrey, they were considered sellouts because they didn't want to blow up the system, because they supported a major party candidate, albeit a liberal Democrat.

At Columbia, every belief I ever held was challenged. It was the height of the debate over Vietnam. We couldn't just operate from certain assumptions and argue about nuances at the margins. Every basic tenet—from capitalism to democracy to societal norms—was up for review. There were bright, serious people willing to contest whatever belief anyone cared to throw out for discussion, and to do so with passion and intelligence. I'd grown up believing wholeheartedly that America was the best country in the world, and that democracy was the only viable system of government, that freemarket capitalism was the best economic system, but there were people at Columbia eager to argue every point. I was bombarded with carefully thought out positions that were totally opposed to my own, by people whose radicalism and dislike of America or promotion of drugs were totally different from anything I'd experienced. Some of my closest friends had Soviet posters on their walls, with the hammer and sickle and the message "Workers of the World Unite!" It was like being transported to another planet; I was assailed by all manner of alien thinking, and I loved it.

For every hour I spent in class or doing outside reading, I spent about nine hours just sitting around and talking. Discussing life. Discussing society. Discussing politics. This, to me, was why I was there, and I tried to make the most of it. I tried to respect even the most outrageous positions, to think through the reasoning behind them and consider whether or not they made sense for our broader society. I tried not to take things personally, and to debate with an open mind, without rancor. It was an intellectually rigorous and emotional exercise, and it offered an invaluable confirmation that I wasn't simply advancing ideas and positions I'd inherited from my family or my community. I was made to fight for every position I held dear, and to reject positions I had taken simply by default.

Our battlefield was the lounge on the second floor of the law school building, just outside the library. There were perhaps eight chairs strewn about the place, and this was where I held forth. Some of my friends called it the Pataki Memorial Lounge, because I was always sitting there. I was either down in Riverside Park, playing basketball, or shooting the bull at the Gold Rail, a neighborhood joint on Broadway where pitchers of beer were only $1.25, or roping whoever was wandering in or out of the library into another endless debate. I rarely made it into the library itself, and went to classes only when I absolutely had to. Who had time for classes? There was the war to consider. It was during my time at Columbia that student deferments were abolished, and we were all suddenly 1-A. Nobody cared about school. Vietnam was all we talked about. We talked about who was over there, we talked about the draft, about the forces in place to put an end to the fighting.

We saw the world through that war, and we saw each other in terms of where we stood. I wasn't opposed to serving my country and fighting to protect our freedom, but I was intensely opposed to the way the Vietnam War was being fought. My feelings were basic: I hated Lyndon Johnson. I thought that what President Kennedy had started—helping the people of South Vietnam to live in democracy, to have religious freedom, and to oppose communism—was absolutely right. But by 1967 it had become apparent that President Johnson was asking American troops to fight with both hands tied behind their backs. The message from Washington was that there was no war. It was guns and butter. This was the opposite of the Gulf War. During the crisis in the Persian Gulf, George Bush took his position to Congress and to the American people. There was a vote; there was public debate—and once the people had spoken, the White House made it plain that we were going to go all-out; there would be a line in the sand and yellow ribbons everywhere and we would be at war.

But back in the 1960s, my friends were being drafted and killed, and still our national government was pretending there was no war. It was preposterous. LBJ was out crowing about his Great Society and his wonderful social programs, but meanwhile 540,000 of our young people were getting shot at without the full resources of the American military behind them. The Johnson administration worked to keep that message from the American public. Clearly, politics dominated the policy. Americans were being killed because of an absurd unwillingness to face up to the fact that we were in a war.

I was completely disgusted—not with the premise that we should oppose communism, but with the way we were doing it. The politicians didn't have the courage to stand up and say, This is what we're doing, and this is why we're doing it. There was no principle that I could see, no leadership. If you think what you're doing is right, and how you're going about it is right, you've got to make the case to the American people. If they agree, then you go out and do what you have to do, what you have the mandate to do. President Bush put his position to a vote before acting on it. You don't talk about your great society and ignore the fact that half a million kids are risking their lives. Either you do it or you don't do it, and the politicians back then were doing it half-assed. It was costing my friends their lives.

There was so much rage and frustration building on college campuses across the country that it's a wonder the students didn't all just implode. Student leaders were itching to rebel and looking for salient issues around which they might incite their campuses to some sort of action. At Columbia, we found ourselves in the midst of a controversy that crystallized the rift between the establishment and the disaffected students. Many people don't remember this, but the dispute leading to one of the most famous campus riots of the era—the one that shut down classes and brought out the police and put the student leader Mark Rudd on the front page of every American newspaper—had nothing directly to do with the Vietnam War. There was a later riot, in 1970, over the bombing in Cambodia, but the one people still talk about took place in 1968, and it was about a gymnasium.

Early in 1968, the university announced plans to build a state-of-the-art gymnasium on public land in Morningside Park, adjacent to the campus. The idea was that the city would lease the parcel to the school, in consideration of which the gym would be made available to the surrounding community on a limited basis. Morningside Park cut right through Harlem, so the "surrounding community" at issue consisted mostly of low-income, apartment-dwelling black families, most of whom had no access at all to the kind of facility Columbia was planning.

On its face, the concept seemed a win-win situation, offering the university a chance to expand beyond the confines of its property and its neighbors a chance to enjoy a fine gymnasium that would not otherwise exist. Nevertheless, some of the more radical students on campus called the plan racist. They dubbed the project "Gym Crow" and criticized university and city officials for using a public park for their own ends. The university made a mistake by designing the gym with one entrance for the university and another for the community. To the students this smelled like the kind of segregation that had kept blacks and whites from drinking water at the same public fountains in some of our southern communities.

Done right, the gym could have been a major asset for both the community and the university. I grew up in a place where there was no gymnasium like the one the university planned. As kids, we rarely had access to a gym. During the winter, there were only two indoor places in Peekskill where we could occasionally play basketball. One was in the basement of the Episcopalian church, which had a makeshift half-court, with pipes stretching across the ceiling in such a way that you had to shoot the ball on a line drive if you wanted it to reach the basket. The other was at the synagogue, where the main dining hall was sometimes converted to a temporary court. I was neither Episcopalian nor Jewish, but once in a while we got to play. We would have been thrilled to have access, even on a part-time basis, to a bonafide gymnasium. We just wanted to play ball, just as some of the kids in Harlem desperately wanted a decent place to play basketball in the winter.

The campus was divided, and the radicals tried to find more to the issue than was really there. I had been active in the Majority Coalition, working to support the university's position, but the radicals held sway. In retrospect, it was no wonder. The tensions over the war mixed with the general antiestablishment air of the times to leave the students in a kind of fever. They were impatient for a chance to rebel, and the gymnasium seemed as good an issue as any. If it hadn't been the gym, it would have been something else.

When the forces finally erupted in a riot, the antiradical Majority Coalition was caught in the cross fire. At first, we'd meant to stand against the protest, but after a while we were swept up in it. Everyone spilled from dorm rooms and apartments to take part—even those who weren't actively involved. In the beginning, there was no violence. It was a tense but peaceful campus happening on a cool spring night. At first, there was just a group of about 1,000 students marching down Amsterdam Avenue from the City College campus, with red banners flying. Then there was Charles 37 X Kenyatta, one of the leaders of the black militant movement in Harlem, marching across 125th Street with another thousand or so of his supporters. And finally there was the Majority Coalition, hastily convened to keep the peace and yet bracing for a pitched battle.

Gradually, things started to percolate. Cries of "Gym Crow must go!" and "Smash the glass of the ruling class!" echoed down the canyons of the wide city streets. Friends of mine—law students!—were marching on Broadway, breaking windows, thinking this would somehow contribute to the debate. I thought everyone was nuts. Before long, the radicals were occupying the administration buildings. Charles 37 X Kenyatta and his people were holed up in Mathematics Hall. And we were on the outside, trying to block the exits so the rioters couldn't get relief.

It was like a war movie, but still there was no outward display of physical violence. Apart from the broken windows, and the unmistakable slow boil of a riot about to happen, it was civil disobedience without incident. There were enough campus and city police around to keep tempers in check, and I remember pausing in the middle of the disturbance to wonder how it would play out, but I couldn't have imagined what happened next: The city's Tactical Patrol Force (TPF) came charging around one of the buildings with arms locked and

clubs out. These were the biggest and toughest New York City police-
men, schooled in riot and crowd control, and over two thousand had
been sent to get control of the situation. (The force has since been dis-
banded.) There was never any order saying "Clear the campus!" or
"Here we come!" or anything. It was plainly stupid, because the TPF
came at the wrong people. The radicals were *inside* the buildings; the
Majority Coalition—supporters of the school—were on the outside,
and we were the ones being chased from the scene. Many of my
friends were clubbed, and I was chased by a cop on a horse all the way
out to Broadway and up to 123rd Street.

It was maddening. We were on the side of the law and the university, and yet no one had taken the time to assess the situation before
moving in. We were all terrified. The police were big men, with helmets, horses, and clubs, running at full speed in a locked line, intend-
ing to bust heads, set an example, and restore the campus to order.
There was nothing to do but flee or be trampled. We had to run, jump
down steps, hurdle the shrubs, and do whatever we could to save our
hides. It was about three o'clock in the morning, and there were
women and young children all around, because until the appearance
of the TPF no one seemed to be in any danger. And then, out of nowhere, the scene erupted into bedlam.

The excessive and arbitrary show of force was alarming. I didn't
see any tear gas, and neither did any of my friends, but some of the
newspaper accounts said tear gas was used. If it was, I'm not surprised. The entire operation was a miscalculation on the part of the police, and what happened was that they radicalized the people who had
supported the university's position. We were clubbed and run down
by horses, and out of sheer frustration many in the Majority Coalition
jumped over to the other side. Or maybe they were just furious. After
all, the radicals were safely inside the administration building; nothing happened to them. It made no sense that we were outside, trying
to quash the uprising, and suddenly being made to run for our lives.

Things went downhill from there. The whole campus fell apart.
Classes were suspended for weeks. Mark Rudd and his crew became a

fixture on the nightly news. When the dust cleared, the gymnasium deal with the city was canceled. Columbia wound up placing its new gym on a corner of the campus that really wasn't large enough to accommodate it; it wound up being less of a facility than it should have been, and the community was denied access. What had been a win-win proposition was transformed into a losing one, and the only victory the radical students could claim was the press they had gotten.

This might have been something, but it came at great cost. One of the problems I had with the radicals was that so many of them just blew with the breeze. They took up whatever cause seemed to fit their needs, and they weren't firm in their convictions. I saw one of them on the subway, not long after graduation. We'd known each other casually in law school; we were both dressed in nice suits and headed downtown to our Wall Street law firms, and I wandered over to say hello. I asked him about his job.

"Oh, it's great," he said. "We have this great dining room that's only for the lawyers."

I couldn't get over his hypocrisy. This man was just a couple of years removed from the time he had run up and down Broadway, chanting, "Smash the glass of the ruling class!" He'd done a 180-degree turn; he valued his new privileged position so much that he couldn't stand to eat lunch with secretaries and paralegals. His attitude struck me as strictly opportunistic, and it reminded me that I had been right to look on those campus protests as a kind of aberration. If everybody's radical, you become a radical to fit in and be one of the crowd. If everybody's an elitist, then you become an elitist and you're part of a new crowd, and damn the consequences to those who don't share your excitement of the moment.

I don't know if I'm in the minority about this one or not, but I'm still affected by the discussions of that period, and the principles, so many of which were positive and altruistic. It was all screwed up, and a lot of the upheaval of the 1960s was malicious and violent, but there was some true altruism, a real desire to make this planet a better place. I loved the concept of sharing and being part of a bigger picture, and I loved the way these notions flowed so freely from our college campuses.

As a result of my own experiences, I came to regard the ivory tower as a sound concept of education. College shouldn't just be about a course of study directly related to a job or career; it should in large part be about intellectualizing and conceptualizing and studying entirely irrelevant and impractical things. For some reason, you're encouraged to think more freely on a college campus, to think without limits. It almost doesn't matter what it is you're thinking about, because you're operating at some remove from the real world. There's an extra layer in place, a protective coating, that allows you to look at issues through an unpolluted lens. In our case, at Columbia, those issues were the Morningside Park gymnasium and the Vietnam War, and in these some found justification to do more than just think. People could throw rocks, march, and occupy administration buildings, and somehow feel that what they were doing was detached from the day-to-day existence they had left at home, the existence they had to look forward to.

I never thought of Columbia as the real world. I just considered it a place filled with extremely bright, passionate people who would someday have a significant impact on the real world. The people I was dealing with could someday be president, or the chief justice of the Supreme Court, or the head of IBM or Greenpeace; and trying to understand their thinking was enormously helpful to me as I tried to understand my own. Gradually, the polarizing issues of my time at Columbia allowed me to see that the principles of my father and grandfather were also mine. I wasn't just echoing their sentiments; I was sounding my own. It was enormously reassuring to have taken my ideas and ideals out for a test drive and felt that they were right.

When students weren't out rioting, debating the issues of the day, or meeting the minimum requirements in our classes, the thing to do at Columbia Law School was to plot a course for a career; but I was still all over the place regarding mine. If politics had seemed important, it seemed so even more with Lyndon Johnson's mishandling of Vietnam. Not only could politicians raise your taxes; they could draft you and send you off to be killed. Having the right people with the right notions hold public offices seemed to me more important than ever. I thought again about teaching. Underneath each prospect was the magnet of home and family—and the farm. I figured that I could go home and be a lawyer and a farmer and maybe run for office when the time was right. I could be like Congressman Gwynn: plant tomatoes, be at home, serve the people, and have the best of it all. Or I could just have the front end—the farm and the family—and still be happy.

All around me, though, as the radicals began to show their elitist colors, the talk on campus was about Wall Street and the huge salaries available to corporate attorneys. I must admit there were times I found myself attracted to the excitement and the possibilities of a big-time law firm. I'd done well at Columbia—made *Law Review*—and knew that a Wall Street job would be easy to come by. The appeal wasn't just the money but the chance to move about in such heady company, to interact with some of the brightest young lawyers in the country, to work on issues that mattered beyond the theorizing of the classroom or one of our political union debates.

I didn't do much to act on that attraction, at least not initially. In my first summer off from Columbia, I went home to Peekskill and worked for a local attorney, a Hungarian contemporary of my father's named Ben Hersh who regaled me with more stories of the Hungarian church than I can now recall. It was time to trade the grueling work of the coal cars at the powerhouse for a more career minded summer job; the Fleischmann's factory was fine for an undergraduate, but it wasn't the best training for a soon-to-be attorney. I earned about $50 per week, and I still got up early to help pick the corn and stayed up late to get the farm stand ready for the next morning.

The next summer I worked at Dewey, Ballantine, a major downtown firm, making about $300 per week. The money was more than I had ever imagined, but in many ways the money was the least of it. I was working on some of the biggest deals in the business world, alongside some of the biggest names. It was an eye-popping experience and an education by fire. My office was on the forty-sixth floor, overlooking the Statue of Liberty. Just sitting there was exciting. I loved it—enough, certainly, to want to go back there after law school. One of the things I kept thinking about was proving myself when it counted. To succeed as a summer associate was one thing, but to go up against these people on a full-time basis, well . . . that was what truly counted. I kept thinking that I needed to test myself, to see if I was as capable as all these other talented, challenging people. A part of me knew that I was, but I wanted validation. I wanted to know that my values were as solid, my judgment as sound, my instincts as sharp as theirs. I wanted to get more of a feel for the place, to see what the big time was really like, before deciding on a fixed course.

Most of my friends were still blue-collar types—young men with values and backgrounds like mine. They weren't necessarily from a farm, or even from a rural area, but they came from strong families with a strong work ethic. I'll never forget one lunch I had with three of them: Tom Carroll, Tom Gallagher, and John Conway.

"My dad was down yesterday," Gallagher said. "It was a great day. He loved my office. He couldn't believe that two months out of law school, I'm already making more than he earned in the last five years."

"Yeah," Carroll added, in a thick Bronx accent, "my old man can't believe I have *any* job."

"Yesterday was one of the best days of my life," Gallagher continued. He explained that his father worked in a foundry outside Boston, making manhole covers. "So there we were," he said, "walking down Wall Street to Broad Street at high noon, all the people out on the street, my father finally in a suit. All of a sudden he gets down on his hands and knees. I looked down and asked him what the hell he was doing. Turned out he stopped to check out a manhole cover, wanted to see if it was one of his." He was proud that his father had done this.

The anecdote served to remind us why we were friends in the first place. Our fathers all worked with their hands. They never went to college. But they worked hard and took enormous pride in their work. That was our common thread. Doing the best you can—as a mailman, a farmer, a steelworker, or a governor—means more than any title or paycheck you can wave before your friends. It all comes from within.

What I found, after Columbia, was that corporate law wasn't really for me—or, if it was, it wasn't where I wanted to be just yet. Initially, I was awestruck by this new environment, and it wasn't just the expensive oriental rugs, the elaborate wood paneling and detailing on the walls, or the custom suits worn by my new colleagues. It wasn't even my starting salary of $15,000, which in 1970 was about three times what my father was earning. It was the atmosphere, the complete package, having to be on top of your game at all times, without letup. I'd played a lot of ball against a lot of truly talented athletes, but this was a level of competition unlike any I had known.

I started out doing estates and litigation, and what I had the most trouble with was the way I had to assume the worst about people. It was something I'd known on an intellectual level, but to have to put it into practice was another matter. To be a good lawyer, in a contract, a real estate deal, or a lawsuit, you have to think in terms of how the other side can take advantage of you. It's your obligation to protect your client, and you do that by anticipating every conceivable worst-case scenario. I wasn't very good at this, because I wasn't practiced at it; it wasn't who I was. To me, growing up in Peekskill, a handshake was as good as any contract, so this sort of maneuvering wasn't part of my thinking; and I saw early on that I could never comfortably be the kind of lawyer I needed to be to succeed in a corporate environment for very long. I liked the people I was dealing with—on both sides of the table—too much not to give them the benefit of the doubt.

It was a whole new mind-set, to sit around over lunch and hear people talk about how they had snookered their opponents and clap each other on the back for this good piece of lawyering. I listened in and tried to convince myself that this was what you had to do, this was what the client expected, but it was a difficult concept. I would have been more comfortable saying to the other side, "Excuse me, but you shouldn't let us have this language in this paragraph because it's not fair to your client." My instincts would have me looking for a fair deal for both sides, but that's not the lawyer's role. Our legal system is built on an adversarial model. True, the adversary system has a lot to recommend it, but I'd rather be a partner than an adversary. I'd rather work in good faith toward a mutually beneficial end than to outsmart my counterparts and deny them something they should be entitled to. I'd rather sleep at night and trust in the belief that people will do what's right, but this was clearly not the way of the big-time world.

So there I was, in these high-pressure surroundings, where top salaries and overachievement were the currency of choice. I learned a great deal, and I made wonderful new friends, but it slowly dawned on me that I couldn't do this forever. I couldn't work in a place where people worried about who had a bigger office or a better title. The things that mattered more and more to the other young associates mattered less and less to me. It got to the point where work wasn't just a matter of beating your adversary; it had become an internal competition as well. I can be as competitive as the next guy, but I like to think I compete over things that matter. My attitude was: If you need the corner office to help you feel important, or the expense account, or the company car, then go ahead and take them; I'm not interested.

I remember being shocked by the fact that most associates spent six or eight years at the firm, at which point they were either up or out. I couldn't understand it. I'd always thought personal relationships were paramount. If you spend the time to get close to people, working with them or living with them, then it's permanent. In retrospect, I suppose the system makes sense. There comes a point where you either achieve something or move on to something else. Either you make partner or you don't. Generally even those who did not make partner parlayed their situation to advantage at another firm. Nothing was permanent in the corporate world, I began to realize. This world wasn't about building for a shared future. It was about doing what you had to do to get ahead, and jumping ship at the first scent of a better opportunity.

Despite all these misgivings, I wound up staying at Dewey, Ballantine for four years, in significant part because we had the best basketball team in the lawyers' league. I wasn't ready to give up this form of competition just yet. We won the lawyers' league championship three of the four years I was there.

Of course, it was more than just basketball that kept me at Dewey, Ballantine. The people I was working with were extremely bright and motivated. I enjoyed many of the day-to-day aspects of my job. I learned a great deal—about estates, litigation, and corporate politics— but mostly what I learned was that I wasn't built to be a Wall Street attorney.

Ultimately, what drew me to politics was politics itself. In the summer before I joined Dewey, Ballantine full-time, I applied for a low-level advance position in Nelson Rockefeller's 1970 gubernatorial campaign. After Yale and Columbia, I'd had enough amorphous political debate and ideological discussion to last a lifetime; I would not have traded those experiences, and I still look back on them as a formative influence in my career, but I had reached a point where I wanted to see what a campaign was like, from the inside, where it counted.

What I found was a revelation. Suddenly, politics wasn't just about making a point; it was about making a change, and a difference. It was about getting out your message and seeing that it took. I absolutely loved it—the seat-of-the-pants excitement, the grassroots enthusiasm— and wondered what had kept me from the real deal for so long. Rockefeller ran a brilliant campaign, with unlimited resources. In many ways, it was an unfair introduction to the world of big-time politics, because the field was so tilted in my candidate's favor, but I was too caught up in the excitement to recognize the imbalance. All I knew, whenever I brought the governor his Oreo cookies and Dubonnet, or handed him a card telling him who would be sitting in at his next meeting, was that I was working to make a difference. All I knew was that when the votes were counted, I might have helped to change a few minds and return the governor to office. And I knew that despite our resources, the basics of our campaign were the same as our opponents'; our nights were just as long, our days just as full.

In truth, I didn't contribute much beyond my youthful zeal to Rockefeller's run for the office I now hold, but what it gave me was incalculable. It taught me, through experience, that anything is possible.

It taught me that it is one thing to stay up late into the night over a couple of beers at Mory's and belabor a point—about welfare, tax reform, the death penalty, or whatever we chose to put on the table—but that it is something wholly different to sell a point to the voting public, to find validation not in whether you've managed to convince your opponent or your friends of your position, but in whether you've persuaded the majority of the people to see things your way.

It was the difference between polemics and democracy, between idea and practice, and it was all the difference in the world.

7

Restoring Freedom
in New York State

THE AMERICAN POLITICAL SYSTEM IS THE RESULT OF THE IN-
credible evolution that began 209 years ago with a four-page
document outlining the limited powers of government and the sacred
or, as Jefferson had referred to it more than a decade earlier, "inalien-
able" rights of the governed. The intent of that document and, in particular, of the Bill of Rights, is clear. It was expressly conceived and
written to ensure that freedom would stand the test of time, and that
the new government the founders created would never grow to be as
powerful and oppressive as the one they had fought to escape.

And so, with the ratification of this document, a new world was
born, based on the idea that government derives its just powers from
the consent of the governed; that government is an instrument of the
people; that government is to be guided by the people; and that government is the people's servant and not their master.

Those values—the values of self-government, democracy, individual liberty, and personal freedom—are America's creation, America's
legacy, America's contribution to the world. But today they are threatened. The threat comes from government and its inherent tendency to

grow larger, more intrusive, more powerful, more expensive, and more burdensome to the taxpayers. As a result of such growth, government still has the power to infringe on the basic freedoms of Americans. Simply by virtue of its size and the amount of money it seizes from taxpayers to keep it running, the federal government is the body by far the most likely to encroach on individual rights and freedoms. This point was underscored during recent congressional hearings revealing countless horror stories of IRS agents running roughshod over the lives of ordinary, hardworking American men and women.

The threat, however, comes from *all* levels of government—federal, state, and even local. Clearly it exists in state government. Since I was elected governor, I've been working to reunite the people of New York with the freedoms stripped from them by Mario Cuomo's government through overtaxation and overregulation. But this threat exists at the lowest levels of government, as well. In my first month as mayor of Peekskill, I was astonished by the excessive parking regulations in effect in the city. I was determined to do a good job and to address some of the substantive issues facing the city over the long term. Certainly I was hoping that my days would be spent on something more meaningful than fixing parking problems. But all I kept hearing, all winter long, were complaints from people about how city regulations forced them to constantly move their cars. On its face, a parking problem might seem like a small thing. But to these people—my constituents— it was a daily inconvenience and, indeed, a major burden. And because this burden was inflicted on them by government, it was my job as mayor to seek to correct the problem. At the state level, the problems were far more severe. One of the prime reasons I decided to run for governor is that I felt New Yorkers were systematically being stripped of their most fundamental freedoms by a government that was out of touch and out of control.

In 1908, when my grandfather was leaving Calabria, tens of thousands of other Calabrians and southern Italians were leaving for America as well. During that period, the Italian government had begun imposing higher taxes on essential items, including the main-stay of rural life: bread. These oppressive taxes placed a heavy financial burden on people, like my grandfather's family, who could least afford it. How ironic, I thought, that my grandfather had left Calabria and come to New York because of oppressive taxes and the lack of opportunity. Now, at the end of the same century, his grandson was seeking to become governor of his adopted state to end oppressive taxes and restore opportunity.

There's no question that high levels of taxation invite fraud, a disincentive to work harder, and a desire to leave for greener pastures. I've seen people throw up their hands and say, "Look, I'm just not going to work if the government is getting 50 percent of every dollar I earn," or "I'll just leave and go someplace else." I understand that; and this is why I will always try to reduce the tax burden on people and return to them the incentive to work harder, produce more, and ultimately generate more revenue for themselves and, incidentally, the government, while expanding economic opportunity.

Remember, government exists to serve the people, not the other way around. Why should you have a 28 percent tax rate, for example, just because people can live with it, if in fact all a sound government really needs is, say, 18 percent? The idea is not to tax people as much as you can get away with, but as little as you need to be successful. If you overtax people or businesses, they'll leave the state. There's simple cause and effect at work here: People will take their families, their factories, or their corporate headquarters and move, and you'll experience a downward spiral, with a smaller private sector left to make up the difference. One of the great things about our republican form of government is that the states compete with one another economically. It's not just one country; it's New York against New Jersey, New York against Connecticut, and if the tax rates are too high in one state, the people will just pack up and move to another. Our fifty states are laboratories of democracy. You can try something in one state, and if it works, another state will copy it; if it doesn't work, another state will benefit from not making the same mistake. Tax policy, welfare reform, economic incentives—the states are becoming free to make their own decisions, their own successes, their own mistakes. This makes for a stronger America.

Perhaps the biggest error our state government leaders can make is to reach for more than they need to conduct the business of government. We in government should be made to do more with less. The burden should be on us, not on the people.

Consistent with that belief, much of my focus since I became governor has been on cutting taxes and regulations. Make no mistake: Overtaxation and overregulation are more than just bad policy; they are an encroachment on people's freedom. By cutting taxes and regulations we are reuniting New Yorkers with the freedoms they lost when government reached too deep into their pockets to pay for more programs and bigger bureaucracies. In my first three years as governor, the impact on our statewide tax cuts was phenomenal. In 1994, Cuomo's last year, New York State had 73 new or expanded corporate facilities. In 1996, we had 511, seven times as many. In 1997, we had 809, more than ten times as many. In just three years we created more than 260,000 new private-sector jobs. And our rate of job growth continues to increase.

Perhaps the clearest example of a job-killing tax had the dubious "honor" of being named after my predecessor. The "Cuomo tax," a transfer tax of 10 percent on all real estate transactions over $1 million, had effectively killed real estate investment in the state over the past decade. If you held a building for years and saw it double in value simply because of inflation, you'd have to give 10 percent of the "gain" back to the state just for the privilege of making the sale; and on top of this, you'd still have to pay income taxes on the gain. The result, obviously, was that people wouldn't invest in New York. Why should they? If you had the choice of a similar property in New Jersey or Connecticut, why would you take on the state of New York as a not-so-silent 10 percent partner?

The Cuomo tax was a classic example of misguided policy. In its first year, it generated more than $800 million in revenues. By the time I took office, that figure had dwindled to about $75 million per year.

The result was clear: If you impose a tax on people who don't have to do business in your state, they're going to take their business elsewhere. Yes, the transfer tax was still raising $75 million, but the loss of revenue from the loss of the investment, renovation, and expansion that would normally spur economic growth and activity was devastating. We were losing investments, losing renovations, and most important, losing jobs. Unemployment in certain construction trades was over 50 percent. It was destructive to the economic climate of the state, and I thought back to Mario Cuomo's remarks when he signed it into law. He called it the "perfect tax."

And as things turned out, he was half right: It was the perfect tax for New Jersey, Connecticut, Georgia, and North Carolina. It was a disaster for New York. And another relic from the Cuomo era shows how preposterous an unchecked government can become. When the legislature had finished imposing new and higher taxes on virtually every breathing and nonbreathing entity within New York's borders, the time had finally come for it to deal with that much-beloved campfire staple: the marshmallow. Now, New York exempts food from sales tax but does not exempt snacks. So, within the halls of Cuomo's bureaucracies, a debate ensued: Is the marshmallow food or is it a snack?

After weeks of wrestling with this bureaucratic dilemma, of such vital importance to New York's future, Cuomo's bureaucrats reached a compromise: If the said marshmallow measures less than one-half inch in diameter, it shall be considered food. If, however, the marshmallow is larger than one-half inch in diameter, it shall then be declared a snack and thenceforth shall be subject to the tax. This is a prime example of too many bureaucrats with too much time on their hands. If they could do this to marshmallows, what would come next? Jelly beans? When I took office, we sent word to the checkout counters that they could put away their rulers. All marshmallows, bulbous or not, were restored rightfully to their rightful, fluffy, tax-free status. This is just one of a thousand silly and senseless regulations we have eliminated. Just as important, we have fought the inevitable tendency of government to grow.

It has been a tough fight. New York's liberal Democrats believed—

and still believe—in more government spending, in higher levels of taxation, and in attacking the "root causes" of crime instead of criminals. They believed—and still do—that an old, failed welfare system that trapped one in eleven New Yorkers in dependence on the government was the right system, and that our reforms are somehow callous.

Quite simply, they're wrong. Freedom comes from living in a safe country. Freedom comes when the government takes less of our money. Freedom comes from having a job, not a government check. Freedom comes when the government is the servant of the people, not its master. That freedom is what brought my grandparents to America and New York. That freedom is what gave them the chance to see their dreams for their children and grandchildren come true. That freedom is what we must preserve, for ourselves, for the next generation, for America.

8

Crime and Punishment

WHEN I WAS GROWING UP, MY REFERENCE POINTS FOR criminal activity were *Dragnet* on television, and Sing Sing prison, down the road in Ossining. The message of *Dragnet* was that if you committed a crime you would be caught and punished. The message of Sing Sing was that television reflected only a watered-down version of society—there were real criminals, just a few miles away. Still, the inmates of Sing Sing did their time in a manner that couldn't quite touch us, just as their crime hadn't quite touched us. It all might as well have been on television.

We never locked our doors when I was a kid. I don't think I had a key to anything until I went away to school. I can still hear the slam of the screen door to our house, the way the springs pulled the door tight to its frame. It was one of the most conspicuous sounds of my childhood, and in summer months it was all we had to keep the world away. The only creatures that screen fortress was meant to keep out were bugs, but even they managed to find their way in.

Criminal violence had no place in my thinking until I was about high school age. Perhaps it should have had a place, given some of the headlines of the day, but it didn't. My friend Paul Greunberger and I used to go down to the city to watch the Mets during our last year in high school. We'd take the train down to 125th Street and the subway back up to the Polo Grounds, and cheer our lungs out for our new favorite team. We could go only to night games, because we were still in school and we had to work on weekends. The problem with the night games, though, was that they ended too late for us to catch a train back to Peekskill. So we'd take the subway down to Grand Central Station after the game, sleep on the benches there, and catch the first train out in the morning. That's how casual we were about security in those days. My parents knew what we had to go through to go to the ball game, and they had no problem with it.

This was surprising, though only in retrospect. My parents—especially my mother—were extremely protective. If I climbed onto a stone wall, she'd be afraid I'd fall off and break my neck; if I stayed out late with friends, she wanted to know where I'd be and with whom. But she never had any trouble with these overnight stays at Grand Central Station. It was just part of the routine. And for all we knew, it was completely safe.

The security I felt I had as a child quickly disappeared after an incident that occurred while I was attending Columbia Law School. During my time there, I was still neglecting even the minor precautions most people took when they ventured off campus. I had brought my Peekskill mind-set with me, and I thought I could go anywhere at any time. I remember walking from 168th Street all the way to 125th Street, through the heart of Harlem, just to look around. I usually did this during the day, but sometimes I walked at night. It was really quite a scene. There were all kinds of vendors lining the street, selling fruits and flavored ices, and I strolled up and down, sampling, thinking about what I was studying in class, enjoying the sights. It was a good way to clear my head; but my roommates all thought I must be out of my head to be walking through Harlem after dark, with no particular destination in mind. I never felt threatened or out of place, but to my friends I was crazy. Perhaps I was.

What happened to end my innocence was that a world-renowned member of the Columbia Law School faculty, Wolfgang Friedman, a professor of international law, was murdered a few blocks north of campus, on his way to the 125th Street subway station, the same one Greunberger and I used at night. Professor Friedman was killed in the middle of the afternoon. The news of his death was troubling enough, but I was even more upset by the reactions of some of my classmates and teachers. People actually wondered, "How dumb could this man have been to walk north of the law school? He should have known better." It was, I heard someone say, "his own fault."

I hadn't known Professor Friedman, but I knew my peers, and I was astonished at the ivory-tower callousness revealed in their responses. I refused to accept that this great scholar had done anything wrong, despite the end result. It just didn't add up. There we were, studying the nuances of criminal law, and the consensus among students and faculty was that Professor Friedman had simply been foolish to head north from the safety of the Columbia campus and into the wilds of Harlem; by some logic, he was responsible for his own murder.

It was a maddening position, but it was widely held, and I began to realize there were two different Americas, one in theory and one in fact. And the most troubling aspect was that most people accepted this; it was okay. We could study the philosophy of criminal law, we could debate defendants' rights and prosecutors' rights and what sorts of information should be allowed into evidence, but underneath that debate should have been recognition of the basic right of law-abiding citizens to walk on their streets or play in their parks without being made to feel their lives are in danger.

There was no connection between what we were studying and the ways we were made to live, and I remember thinking there was a horrible injustice in this. A philosophically sound argument on a fine point of criminal law was irrelevant to the ability of people to live in safety in their own communities, and it pointed out the hypocrisy in the liberal approach to crime in this country. Liberals could talk all they wanted about our allegedly oppressive society, about the need for rehabilitation in our prisons, about the argument for leniency in sentencing, but none of this offered any of us a free pass on our neighborhood streets.

The general response to the tragic death of this man made me think about the death penalty and the consequences of violent criminal acts. I'd considered this before—in high school debates, in talks around the family bacon roast, in late-night arguments at Yale over beer and pizza—but never in such real terms; and now that I was forced to ponder it, I discovered my position waiting for me, resolutely.

When you're dealing with people who have no respect for human life and yet still fear for their own, you must do what you can to save the lives of those who obey the law. That's justice. It's basic. It's the best we can do as a society—and the least we can do to help the victims' families find a kind of peace.

One mother whose daughter was murdered put it succinctly: "That killer's mother visits him in jail," she said. "I visit my daughter at the cemetery. It's not right."

No, it's not.

I was raised to believe that if you go out and wantonly murder someone, absent some special circumstances, then you forfeit your own right to go on living. It wasn't something I intellectualized or reduced to an "eye-for-an-eye" argument. It was just an issue of right and wrong, and I came to look on the death penalty as an integral part of a system of justice that invariably serves as a deterrent to anyone who might make the cold-blooded decision to take another life. It is symbolic to those considering the act and punitive to those who've committed it.

Under Mario Cuomo, New York's criminal justice efforts seemed to have been aimed primarily at rehabilitation, at prisoners' rights, at shouldering responsibility for those who had taken the wrong path. It was such nonsense. The only priority, to my thinking, was to keep the bad guys behind bars and give the good guys back their streets and their parks. While the rhetoric of Cuomo called for compassion for the poor, it was precisely in our poorest communities where Cuomo's policies led to the highest incidence of violent crime. It was the children in Harlem and Bedford-Stuyvesant and the worker who rode the subway and then walked home at the end of the midnight shift who were at greatest risk. People who lived in buildings with doormen and in gated communities could afford to show compassion for criminals. Those who could not flee their crime-ridden neighborhoods paid the price for others' compassion.

And therein lies one of the biggest challenges I've faced as governor: getting the state legislature to embrace what, for most people, is an incredibly simple principle—that criminals cause crime.

It sounds ludicrous when you phrase it like that. After all, who would dispute the point that criminals cause crime? No one would say it quite like that. Unfortunately, there are those whose philosophy on how to treat criminals and crime is essentially grounded in the misguided logic that criminals are really not responsible for their behavior. Instead of placing *all* the blame where *all* the blame belongs—with the criminal—they seek to hold society partly culpable, claiming that the criminal's actions are a result of social factors beyond his control. They refer to these factors as the "root causes" of crime. I refer to it as nonsense.

I am not blind to the fact that certain social factors—and certainly poverty is one of them—can have a negative impact on people in ways that *conceivably* could make them more susceptible to engaging in negative behavior. But there are too many bright, talented, and successful people rising from squalor to greatness to support the view that poverty produces only criminals.

The root causes of crime are the criminals who engage in it. And during my tenure as governor, I've repeatedly made that point to the legislature. And I've also made it clear to the members of that distinguished body—in no uncertain terms—that we, as servants of the people, are not charged with carrying out a sociological study; we are charged with maintaining public order and saving lives. It is our highest obligation to the people we serve.

Pursuant to that undisputable fact, it is clear that the only way to "eliminate the root causes of crime" is by *arresting* the root causes of crime, *prosecuting* the root causes of crime, and *keeping* the root causes of crime in prison, where they belong. It all goes back to the fundamental principle best summed up by the writer Ben Wattenberg, who observed, "A thug in prison can't mug your sister." Of course, not everyone shares that seemingly obvious observation. Following my 1998 State of the State Address, a story in the *Albany Times-Union* offered a completely different view from a so-called expert in the area of crime. This individual flatly rejected the idea that tougher laws have anything to do with New York's declining crime rates. Instead, he attributed the drop in crime to, among other things, a truce between rival gangs. Somehow I must have missed the news conference where they announced this historic peace accord.

Despite the views of the "experts," in three years we've seen a direct correlation between tougher, commonsense laws and lower crime rates. Today, New York has stronger laws and, not by coincidence, fewer victims.

Indeed, my very first initiative as governor was to return the death penalty to New York State. It had been a major issue of the campaign, a kind of litmus test distinguishing me from my opponent. People have suggested that those who support the death penalty are somehow wavering in their support of human life in general, but to me the position actually suggests quite the opposite: I have such enormous respect for the sanctity of life that I cannot tolerate the taking of life. If you cross that line, if you choose to kill someone as a part of a calculated criminal act, then you no longer deserve to be judged by the same standards as the rest of us. I don't have the slightest doubt about the propriety or correctness of that statement.

People often ask if I won't feel guilty the first time a death sentence is carried out in New York under the new law, if the punishment won't in some way haunt me on a personal level. But I honestly don't think it will. It hasn't happened yet, so I can't be sure, but I expect that when it does, it will register as justice being served. That's all. My administration has sought the death penalty in several cases, but the state has yet to try one of those cases to conclusion. In at least two instances, the suspects killed themselves; in the others, the defendants have accepted life sentences without parole in exchange for pleading guilty.

In one high-profile case, we were able to extradite a convicted murderer, Thomas Grasso, to Oklahoma, where he'd been sentenced to death. The case became a big issue in the 1994 gubernatorial campaign, after Grasso admitted killing an eighty-two-year-old man in Staten Island by winding a television cord five times around the victim's neck. He also admitted strangling an eighty-seven-year-old woman in Tulsa on Christmas Eve, using the extension cord for the lights from her holiday tree and then smashing her skull with a piece of wood.

Mario Cuomo maintained that Grasso had to serve his life sentence in New York before he could be sent back to Oklahoma, where he had already been convicted of murder and faced death upon return. How stupid was that? There was no reason to keep him here, other than the fact that Cuomo was morally opposed to the death penalty. Grasso himself thought he deserved to die. So did his parents. His mother told reporters that she had raised her son to take responsibility for his actions. "If you buy your ticket, you take your ride," she said.

Cuomo was so keenly aware of the senselessness of his position— serve a life sentence in New York, and then go back to Oklahoma to be executed—that even he couldn't make the argument. So he simply said New York State was required by law to keep Grasso for the length of his sentence. It wasn't. When I took office, most of the records pertaining to the Grasso case had been destroyed, but we were able to find one document in which Cuomo's counsel had outlined the legal ways for the state to send Grasso back to Oklahoma. And so we did. He was executed two months later.

The press in Albany asked for my feelings on the matter for about a week leading up to it. "He's gonna be killed tonight, Governor," a reported asked, "doesn't that bother you?"

It didn't bother me, except for the fact that it had taken so long. I probably shouldn't say that, but I can't shy away from the truth. The man was an admitted murderer who himself said he deserved to die. I didn't kill Thomas Grasso by sending him back to Oklahoma. He did it to himself. He strangled that woman with her own string of Christmas lights, and then he stole four dollars in pennies from her bureau and laughed about it. He killed that man from Staten Island and then stomped on his face.

All I did was see that justice was served.

Of course, the best way to see that justice is served is by denying criminals the opportunity to commit crime in the first place. In New York, we're doing this. We've ended parole for repeat violent felons. We've doubled the minimum sentence a violent felon must serve. We've ended early release and work release for violent felons.

But all of the laws in the world are meaningless if, behind each law, there's a technicality that prevents police from enforcing it. No criminal justice system—in *any* state—is perfect. The difference between our state and others is this: The imperfections in *our* system almost always benefit criminals. There's a huge difference between a *fair* trial and a *perfect* trial. Ours is the only state that mandates a purely perfect trial.

In three years, we've taken great strides in restoring sanity to New York's courtrooms by eliminating the absurd legal technicalities created by liberal judges that allowed guilty criminals to escape justice— like the one that enabled a defendant to skip his court date, and then claim that his right to a speedy trial was violated.

And these changes are working. Today, New York's rate of homicide is the lowest it's been since the 1960s. In just three years, the state's murder rate has been cut nearly in half. Today, New York is the safest large state in America, and for two years running, our rate of decline in violent criminal activity has been twice the national average.

By attacking crime at its *true* roots, New York is winning the war against crime. At the same time, we know that we can't be content with reducing crime. When it comes to protecting lives, we can only be content with absolute success. No level of crime is acceptable. That is why we must fight to end parole for all violent felons and get tough on violent juvenile criminals. We must restore dignity and hope for all New Yorkers. But the message is clear: Getting tough on criminals is more than just political rhetoric; it works. Our streets are safer. Our homes are stronger. Our future is brighter.

There is no reason why the peace and security I felt as a child cannot be shared by all New Yorkers, for all time. I long for my kids to grow up in the relative safety I enjoyed as a kid, and even to return to that security myself, but until we get there I content myself in knowing that the world is relatively safer than it was just a few years ago, and that it will be safer still in the future.

9

Family

I SMASHED INTO MY FUTURE WIFE, LIBBY, IN THE SUMMER OF 1971, on the shores of Long Island. Our two worlds collided, quite literally, in the foam of a violent wave: We were thrown helplessly against each other on a sandbar just off Tiana Beach, in East Quogue.

It sounds corny in the retelling, but it's true. Still, it was the kind of chance meeting that makes a better story in retrospect than it did at the time. You had to do a bit better than hit me over the head with fate for me to recognize it; a full-body check was about what it took—and even then I couldn't be sure there was anything more to the collision than a happy accident.

We were bodysurfing, in the prestorm insanity of a serious-weather advisory, lured by the phenomenal waves and the fact that the beach was closed to bathers. The latter was not surprising. There was a genuine hurricane brewing off the North Carolina coast, the waves at Tiana Beach were humongous, and it was dark and cloudy. It wasn't actually raining, but the skies were ominous. Still, a sandbar had formed about a quarter mile from shore, and it was the kind of sandbar we didn't see more than every other year or so; to ignore it would have been an abomination to an experienced bodysurfer. You see, when the truly giant waves break along a sandbar, you don't get dumped on the hard pebbly surface of the shoreline; rather, you're returned gently to the sandy bottom and encouraged to get back out and try another ride. Oh, you still might get dumped, but it's a much more reasonable landing, and my friends and I listened to the warnings of the lifeguards and thought, Yeah, right.

Libby Rowland, bless her, had thought pretty much the same thing. After a couple of rides, I noticed an unfamiliar head bobbing in the waves out there with us, and I thought how strange and wonderful it was to have this brave and crazy girl in our midst. She was tall and thin, tan and healthy, and she struck me as being in remarkably good shape; she was taking as many waves as we were and giving them all a good, strong ride, and I remember looking on and wondering why I'd never seen her before. She was as out of her head as any of us, to be out bodysurfing in this prehurricane.

Before I could attempt one of my lame opening lines, a wave caught us both unprepared and threw us to the ground in a tangle of limbs and sand. This was my opening, and reason enough to meet on the beach for a beer when we were through, but that was all it might have been. Over the course of the summer, however, we kept bumping into each other—on dry land, at the supermarket, on the beach with mutual friends—and when we did we talked about that extraordinary day on the waves. It was our first piece of shared history, and there would be about a million more.

This was the summer of 1971, after my first year at Dewey, Ballantine, and a group of my new colleagues and old friends from law school had gone in on a share house in East Quogue, at $150 each. There were fourteen of us spending our weekends in a two-room shack, which seemed to us about the best we could do, and more than we deserved. Quogue itself was a fashionable community—perhaps the first showy East End town on the way to the Hamptons—but East Quogue back then was the kind of place where you'd find roosters and chickens in the street. It was just our speed. We were so completely out of the social scene that we didn't know we were out of the social scene. We never went to any fancy parties because we were never invited to any. (We hardly even heard about any.) We didn't know there were places to go where you were supposed to be seen. We just had a great time, on the cheap—bodysurfing, playing basketball, going out and drinking beer and dancing all night long.

By Labor Day weekend, we finally caught on to what we were missing and decided to crash a beach party in the Hamptons. We weren't invited, but everyone on the beach was talking about it and we figured we'd go. It was a bring-your-own-booze sort of affair, and we weren't about to show up empty-handed. But we didn't want to dip into our hardly deep pockets to spring for any brand of liquor these hosts would consider serving, so we collected the empty sangria bottles we'd drunk over the course of the summer, put them in a case, and passed them off as our contribution. We didn't even bother to re-fill the empty bottles with water, thinking that would just make them too heavy and that probably no one would notice. It was a good move. The man at the gate just looked at the case and waved us in.

Libby was there, with a date, and I was hanging around with an-other girl, but we still managed to talk for a half hour or so. I really liked her, and for some reason Libby didn't find me too objectionable. We talked a little while about our families and our dreams. She gave me her address. She was going off to college the next day—her first se-mester at Clark University, in Worcester, Massachusetts, after two years at the American College of Paris—and I promised to drop her a note to see if she was settled.

The first time I invited Libby Rowland out on a date was to the Harvard–Yale game that fall. It was the tradition, among our crowd, to go back to New Haven or Cambridge every year for the football game and to act horribly. We were young adults, looking ahead to a lifetime of responsibility and restraint, so the Harvard-Yale game loomed on the calendar as our one opportunity to behave like the overgrown chil-dren we had until recently been. Here again, Libby seemed not to mind. (Or, at least, she was a good sport.) I picked her up at the New

Haven train station, with my friend and Yale roommate Mac Hansing in his falling-apart car, with his two giant dogs slobbering in the backseat, and she hopped right in as if it were a chariot sent to take her to a royal ball.

Yale was beaten badly, by five or six touchdowns, but we cheered every two-yard gain. All through the game, people kept looking at us as though we were nuts, because we were whooping it up while our team was getting killed down on the field, but we didn't care. We were just having fun—Libby, too. We went out dancing all that night, at different parties around campus, and in the middle of it all it occurred to me that Libby had now seen me at my worst—bodysurfing in a storm at Tiana Beach, sneaking into a party with a case of empties, carrying on with my crazy Yale roommates—and yet she still liked me.

I thought, This isn't so bad. It truly wasn't, and she has now seen me in even more unflattering circumstances. On the face of it, we must make an odd pair. Libby's family has a fascinating history, and when you stack it up against mine it's positively worldly. On her father's paternal side, the Rowlands have been in Connecticut since 1638; on her father's maternal side, they've been in Virginia since Jamestown. She's a direct descendant of Henry Percy, the first earl of Northumberland, later immortalized in Shakespeare's *Henry IV* as Hotspur (for his readiness to ride off into combat). Her father's family was both Yale and military to the core. Her father's grandfather was General Sherman's nephew. He was sixteen during the Civil War, and it fell to him to round up a herd of cattle and drive it down to Georgia to help supply his uncle.

Libby's father, Colonel Henry Rowland, graduated from Yale and joined the Army in 1938. He was one of the first American officers sent to North Africa during World War II, principally because he spoke French as well as he spoke English. After some heroics, he became the youngest American colonel, commanding the first combat engineers. He took to his position with the bearing of someone who knew no other way of life; for generations, the men in his family had led other men in battle.

His own father, Libby's grandfather, had been an Army doctor, stationed in the Philippines with General Patton's father, who was also a medical officer. There, Libby's grandfather taught the young Patton to sail—a link to some of Colonel Rowland's favorite stories. In one, he found himself in North Africa, where he was joined by General Patton about a week before beating back an attack led by the German commander, Erwin Rommel. The story my father-in-law tells is that General Patton called him over and reminded him that his father, Libby's grandfather, had taught Patton to sail. "It's good to have another gentleman in the Army," Patton said, and they shared a drink.

When Rommel's men had broken through the Allied lines, and the colonel's combat engineers held as the last line of defense against the Germans, the general continued to treat Libby's father with honor and good cheer. He stood at the colonel's side and respectfully suggested to his great family friend that he open fire.

"No," the colonel replied. "We'll wait until they're a little closer."

When the Germans were a little closer, Patton tried again. "Now?" he said.

"No," Libby's father insisted. "We'll wait."

At this point, the German soldiers were very nearly on top of the engineers, and General Patton turned to Colonel Rowland and commanded him to fire. Unfortunately for General Patton, he did this in earshot of General Alexander, a British general who was the overall commander of the mission.

General Alexander countermanded Patton's order. "I've been fighting with the colonel for the last few months," he explained. "You've just been here a week. He opens fire when he wants to."

And so they waited, ultimately routing Rommel's troops and leading a counterattack across the desert. It was a huge victory for the Allies, and before the battle was over General Alexander turned to Colonel Rowland and congratulated him on his patience and timing. He promised Rowland the highest possible decoration.

Patton, though, was incensed at the open challenge to his authority, and he was not nearly so charitable. He looked at Colonel Rowland, noticed that his shirt had been torn by some shrapnel, and announced that he was out of uniform. "If you're not in proper uniform in a half hour," he said, "I'm going to have you court-martialed."

In the end, Libby's father received the Order of the British Empire, which was only rarely awarded to American officers, as well as the French Legion of Honor. Patton never spoke to him again.

I held Libby's rich family history up against mine and appreciated the difference. (It sounded like the Szoniczs and Patakis in Aranyosa-pati again.) But Libby appreciated all the things she'd missed in her own growing up. She loved the ways we were connected to the land, and to each other. She loved the fact that the Rowlands had been here for centuries and that we were right off the boat. She loved that I came from a big, sprawling family, and that while her large family had been scattered all over the globe, mine had managed to stay relatively put; we may have arrived later on American shores, but we weren't going anywhere just yet.

Somehow Libby and I found enough to like about each other to embrace the differences in our backgrounds and look ahead to some kind of future. What that future held was not entirely certain, but there was the appeal of knowing we would face it together. Too, there was an unsolicited promise, from me to Libby, that we'd live in New York City. As much as I loved the idea of returning to Peekskill as a kind of country lawyer, farmer, and would-be politician, I loved the idea of being joined to Libby even more, and I couldn't see consigning her to the conventional pace of small-town living after her exciting life abroad. She had lived in Korea and France; indeed, she had spent most of her life in Paris, and I knew that the only things Peekskill and Paris had in common was the first letter of their names. Her mother's family had lived in Morocco. Libby never came right out and asked if I had any notion of returning to the farm one day, but I thought that for some reason she might object, so I gave her my preemptive word.

A lot of good that did her.

We lived in Manhattan, at first, in a rent-controlled one-bedroom apartment on West 70th Street. It was a good deal: $175 per month, right off Central Park, in the middle of all kinds of excitement. We used to go out every night—to eat, to drink, to make merry. We were typical wasteful young professionals, making more than we deserved and spending more than we made.

We could have stayed on West 70th Street forever, were it not for our dog, Rathbone. We had gotten into the habit of going up to Peekskill on weekends. Libby really took to my family and to the farm. It was quite a contrast from the farming she had known in France. Her grandfather, a doctor, was a gentleman farmer. He had a big manor house, with a cook. We were dirt farmers. Luxury on the Pataki spread meant heat and running water, but Libby fit right in. Grandpa Pataki had died the year before Libby and I met, but Grandma still lived in the original house, which was all but falling down around her. I took Libby to meet her, and Grandma spoke to me conspiratorially, in Hungarian.

"What's her name?" she asked.

"Elizabeth."

Grandma thought about this a moment and smiled, for it was her name as well. "She's very pretty," she finally said, "but can she work?"

We took the train up with Rathbone almost every weekend, and as the dog grew bigger the conductor grew less tolerant of his behavior. It was fine when he was a puppy, but when the mutt grew to almost four feet long he started chasing after every pet on the train. He behaved awfully (he was, after all, a dog), so we finally had to leave him on the farm with my parents and visit him on weekends. We convinced ourselves that Rathbone would be happier there, with the farm as his playground.

Gradually, we convinced ourselves that we would be too. By this time, Grandma had moved into my parents' house, so Libby and I started using my grandparents' house—on weekends, at first, but soon enough full-time. There was no heat, no toilet, no shower. We were able to manage with these accommodations when it was just the two of us, and just once in a while, but there were forces at work other than Rathbone, so we set about rehabilitating the place. In this, my father was a big help. He was handy himself, but he knew a carpenter who could do this and a plumber who could do that; he signed on as our general contractor of sorts. His friends wouldn't take any money for helping us out, but at the end of the day they went home with a bushel of apples or a couple of bottles of wine. Dad even had a friend who worked in the water department, who came by on weekends to fix the water lines, and someone who could put tar paper on the roof and help patch the leaks. Nothing was done professionally, but everything was done enthusiastically, and done just well enough to suit us.

At around this same time, I had the good fortune to work for Bernie Gordon, our state senator from Peekskill, and I was struck once again by the possibilities of state government. Senator Gordon was chairman of the Senate Judiciary Committee, and chairman of a Joint Legislative Task Force on Court Reorganization. We were both from Peekskill; his daughter had been a year behind me in junior high school; we were both pretty much on the same page, politically and personally.

Bernie Gordon was an outstanding public servant and a passionate role model. He truly cared about the people in his district, which at that time covered most of Westchester and Putnam counties. (It's since been redistricted, with southern Westchester lopped off in favor of a big chunk of Dutchess County to the north.) He always took 70 percent of the vote, and yet he worried constantly about his popularity. He never took his position for granted, and we both understood that the most popular elected official can still be defeated. With every political race, I start out by thinking, What if I don't win? Where will I be? What will I do? I don't believe you can remain as effective in government as you hope to be without thinking through what your life would look like if you left. It gives you the luxury to do what your principles and vision dictate.

Senator Gordon invited me to join his task force, and I grabbed the opportunity. In New York State government, temporary commissions have a life span of about a century, so I figured I could take a leave from Dewey, Ballantine, do some good work over the next few years, and use the time to consider my next move. It wasn't as though I were going to another firm. I was leaving on good terms, and I could always go back if politics, or Peekskill, turned out not to be what Libby and I were looking for.

And those few years would not be spent simply biding my time. We did some good, enterprising work. His task force created the Office of Court Administration, to consolidate and centralize the unified court system in the state; and we passed a constitutional amendment providing for an appointed court of appeals, as opposed to an elected court. These were both very dramatic changes. Indeed, when I became governor, the chance to make my first appointment to the court of appeals flowed directly from the work we had done on the commission.

Peekskill was not Manhattan, and practicing law in Peekskill was nothing like being in a Wall Street firm, but this seemed the perfect transition from the big time to the small-town life I thought I wanted. I spent a lot of time in Albany, seeing state government in action, and I fell in love with the excitement of it. Right away, I recognized that state government was much more directly relevant to the quality of life in our communities than the federal government. Decisions made at the state level had a direct impact on people's lives; decisions made at the federal level were sometimes so diluted by the time they reached the people that the intent was obscured.

As a result, I started to lose the excitement I once felt about Washington, D.C. So many of my friends with political ambitions were looking for federal appointments, but I kept looking homeward and thinking that I could make a big difference with small strokes. I tried to root my hopes realistically. Governor was not a realistic goal, I thought at the time. Nelson Rockefeller was governor. Franklin Roosevelt was governor. Averell Harriman was governor. Over the past hundred years, almost every governor of New York had come from a background of wealth or important connections. As a mailman's kid from a rocky Peekskill farm, I had neither, but I figured I would have a chance for one of the most powerful positions in Albany—majority leader of the state senate. In that position I would be able to advance the policies and ideas I believed in. That became my goal, and as I worked with Senator Gordon over the next few years I tried to get a feel for the capital and chart a course for my first run for office. When the time came, I wanted to be ready.

We still kept our apartment in the city during this period of treading water, even though we spent most of our time on the farm. Libby had taken a job in the international department at Paine Webber, in the same building as Dewey, Ballantine, so we flip-flopped in our commuting schedule. Just as she started heading down to Wall Street every day, I started heading up to Peekskill or Albany. We met in between, most nights, for dinner.

It wasn't a great way to live, but it was manageable until we could figure out our next move. In the meantime, we continued fixing up my grandparents' house. One of my roommates from law school, Steve Weiner, had some bungalows in the Catskills, and he knew how to put in a water heater, so I invited him down and he helped me out. We used gas fittings, which any plumber will tell you should not be used for running water; but we didn't know how to do the welding for the plumbing pipes, and the gas fittings worked fine. We put in a shower. We still used the outhouse, which was charming in a rustic sort of way, unless the weather was cold or otherwise bad; in that case, we'd cross the yard to my parents' house to use their basement facilities; they left the basement door open, so we could go in style.

When friends came to visit on the weekends, they couldn't believe how we lived. At first, they couldn't get over the outhouse, but by nightfall they were willing to forget the lack of plumbing, because the frigid temperatures were so much worse. It was so cold in winter you could freeze to death, without exaggeration. There was no heat, no insulation. The house was just plank boards, and if the temperature was thirty degrees outside the house, it was perhaps thirty-two degrees inside the house. One night, a friend's dog jumped into bed with us, shaking violently. (It was a big, fat, furry beast—one of the two that had gone with me to meet Libby at the station for our first Harvard–Yale game.) I thought the animal was having a stroke, but she was just cold. We didn't chase her out, because once she warmed up a bit she kept us warm, too.

I don't know how my grandparents had managed all those years. They had it a little better, I suppose, because they had some heat from the wood-burning stove in the kitchen; but by the time we moved in, the iron grate had been burned through so that we couldn't stoke up the fire and leave it to burn all night long. We could fire up the stove during the day, but at night we got by on residual heat, body warmth, and extra blankets. It was that or take down the door and burn it.

Libby decided to leave Paine Webber before we started a family. She wanted to stay at home, get the house ready, and think about being a mother. We were alike in this way. I didn't want to seek my first elected office without thinking it through, and she couldn't see starting a family until she had spent some time with the idea; when the time came, she too wanted to be ready.

Peekskill quickly became home for Libby, just as it had always been for me. It sneaked up on her. We never sat down and said, Okay, let's make this move; let's make our lives here. One day she woke up and found herself in the middle of a routine: She'd get up early, around six, and run over to my parents' house to take a shower. (We, of course, didn't have one.) My father would have breakfast waiting when she was through: two poached eggs on toast, no butter, with a pinch of paprika and a cup of coffee. Then she went out and tended to what had been my grandmother's flower garden—a small square, maybe twelve feet by twelve feet, tucked between the western side of the house and a natural stone wall. She worked the garden every morning that first spring and uncovered all the original flower plantings and brought them back to life. My uncle John used to bring my grandmother a lily every Easter, and she'd plant the lily; Libby was able to find most of the lilies and get them flowering again. She planted little rosebushes. She had a vision in her head of a perfect little garden. The flowers had been my grandmother's pride and joy, and now they were Libby's as well.

One day, we looked up and our lives were there waiting for us. We were home. There was new wallpaper; there was a fresh coat of paint; there were Libby's beautiful flowers. Sitting on the porch you could look west out over the fields to the Hudson Highlands, on both sides of the Hudson River. It had just happened, but it felt right. The thing that moved us from our loose plans and my work on the judicial task force was the chance to make a real impact in our community, to matter, to have what Congressman Gwynn once had. It was also time.

We'd both come from large families—Libby with her five siblings, and I with my brother and all my cousins—and we both looked forward to having a lot of children. Of course, we couldn't raise a family in that tiny, drafty house, but there was no need to move until we were under way. We were still there when Emily, our oldest, was born in 1979; but a house became available soon afterward, on what had been my other grandfather's property, adjacent to the Pataki farm. It was the house my mother's sister and her husband used to live in—my aunt Nan and uncle Ozzie—but my cousins had asthma, so they had to sell and move to Arizona for relief. Here, twenty years later, we finally had a chance to buy it back into the family. It was a fantastic spot, tucked into the back corner of the farm, right next to the city reservoir. I could go out the back door and jog through the orchards, down past our farm stand, past Grandma's house, and back up through the grapevines to our backyard. It cost us all of $40,000.

Teddy joined Emily in 1982, and then Allison followed in 1985; Owen rounded us out in 1987. It worked out well: girl-boy-girl-boy, and Libby and I used to sit with our big family under the apple tree in back of our house and think that there was no other place in the world.

In 1978, while I was still contemplating my future, I worried that my too-careful thinking had gotten me into a hole. Senator Gordon had been stricken with cancer and died quickly, and a young Republican assemblywoman named Mary Goodhue was elected to the state senate from our district. It suddenly seemed unlikely that I'd wind up in her seat anytime soon, so I went back to practicing law part-time, working with Libby and my father the rest of the time to get the farm back up and running. Our lives, our time, our family history, were all now linked, again, to Peekskill, and we didn't like what we saw. Local Republicans didn't like it much either, and after a while some of our friends and neighbors started looking to me to do something about it.

"George," I'd hear, at least a couple times each week, "why don't you run for mayor?"

Being mayor of Peekskill would be a difficult, time-consuming job, if it was done right. No one had ever gone on to anything after being mayor of Peekskill, and it would have been foolish, perhaps even arrogant, to think I'd be any different. Still, the idea was not without its appeal. Libby and I wanted to make a commitment to the farm and to the community, but we were disappointed by what was happening to Peekskill; its leadership had left us with a rising crime rate, rising taxes, and a rising vacancy rate that together made pockets of the city seem like a desolate ghost town. The city's Hungarian flavor was mixed, as it had always been—with Irish, Polish, Italian, Hispanic, Slovak, African-American, and now even Asian influences—but much of the factory work had disappeared. According to the 1980 census, 35 percent of Peekskill's population had government assistance as their primary means of support. Where there was once opportunity, there was now a shared struggle to get by. It hardly resembled the Peekskill I'd known as a kid—the people seemed to lack confidence or faith in tomorrow—and I couldn't see any kind of turnaround on the horizon.

And so we faced a family question: Do we pack up, sell out, and move someplace else, as a great many of our family and friends had done, or do we try to change things? Had it not been for the farm, we probably would have left. After all, you can't take a farm with you, and our farm was a unique part of our family history, a living link to what my grandfather had started; and now that he was gone, we didn't want to lose such a precious heirloom. It was, for us, the entire legacy of two generations in America—and, we hoped, a third generation.

We decided to stay, and it fell to me to deal with changing things in Peekskill. Libby and my family would run the farm, and I would see about running the city, if the people of Peekskill would have me. I wasn't sure they would. In 1981, Peekskill was a largely Democratic town of about 20,000; it was still a working-class town, except that there wasn't as much work as there used to be—certainly, there wasn't always enough to go around. The downtown area, once a thriving center of community life, now had abandoned buildings and decaying storefronts; it hardly looked like a place where anyone would want to come and start a business or raise a family.

Politically, a Republican hadn't won anything in Peekskill in years, but I still believed in the people, most of whom I knew by name. It wasn't their fault that the city was in decline; it was, I came to believe, the fault of a lackadaisical government that had not inspired the people with ideas or offered viable candidates who could make a difference. As a first step, I became Republican city chairman—this was not difficult in a Democratic town—and in 1979, we scored our first real breakthrough, electing Richard Jackson to the city council. Dickie, my closest friend since the fourth grade, was the first Republican on the city council since Watergate and the first African-American ever elected to any office in Peekskill. There were many six-to-one votes on the city council, with Richard Jackson cast in the role of loyal opposition, but his voice gave us a platform for ideas about reenergizing Peekskill. The problem was that all we had was a platform; with only one representative on the council, we couldn't implement anything, and I started to realize that in order to achieve real success we needed to put together a strong team.

And so, in 1981, I finally entered my first political race, hoping to unseat the incumbent, Jay Bianco. I recruited the best running mates I could find to sit on the city council. Vinnie Vesce was the key. A lifelong resident from a prominent local family (his father was the family doctor for half the town), Vinnie was also president of our Christopher Columbus Club, perhaps the most influential civic association of the most influential ethnic group in town. Vinnie had been a good friend of mine since junior high school, and he'd just written a letter to the newspaper criticizing some of the stupid decisions of the current administration, and I knew right away he was my man. I sought him out at the Christopher Columbus Club one winter Tuesday night, at one of the club's bimonthly social dinners.

"Vinnie," I said, "how are you?"

"Good, George," he said. "What're you up to?"

"Not much. Thinking about running for mayor."

Vinnie looked stunned. "Mayor?" he asked. "What the hell? Jay's the mayor. Everyone likes him here."

I'd expected as much. "Yeah," I tried, "but what do *you* think?"

"Me? I don't do politics. Personally, I think they're all inept at City Hall. They don't have a clue."

"I know," I said. "I saw your letter. That's why I'm thinking of running. I think I can win. I think I can change things, start to turn the city around. I think you'd be the perfect guy to help."

"Run for office?" Vinnie shot back. From his reaction, it was clear he'd never even entertained the notion. "As I said, George, I don't do politics. I'm not that dumb. I've got a great job. I don't just commute to the city every day. I go all over the world."

"I know," I said. "That's why we need you. What are you, anyway? Republican or Democrat?"

"Italian," he said. "I'm not anything, but I'll tell you what, Jay or no Jay, run and I'll back you. These guys are ruining this city."

I called Vinnie every day for the next week, telling him we could make a difference, win the election, and along the way have a heck of a good time.

In the end, Vinnie not only backed me, but ran alongside me; and he eventually succeeded me as mayor, after Richard Jackson, to continue our efforts to transform Peekskill. With Vinnie, Ed Creem, and Chuck Miller, two other people with no political experience but a fine record of community service, we set off on our crusade. That's all it was, and all it might have been, but our message of change seemed to sweep the city, and I wound up tallying more than twice as many votes as my opponent.

I came away from that election with a tremendous sense of pride and gratitude. I was even somewhat in awe of the job. Now that I am governor, it seems strange to me that I considered the job of mayor of Peekskill to be a daunting or challenging task. But I did. I knew that I hadn't just won. I knew that thousands of ordinary people, seniors living on social security, immigrants barely able to speak English, workers who didn't want to lose their jobs to North Carolina or Texas . . . these good people had given me their vote and their trust. I was grateful; but, more than that, I was determined to produce.

Being mayor of Peekskill was probably the hardest job I've ever had, except for working the coal cars at the Fleischmann's factory. It paid $6,750 per year for more than 90 hours of work per week—without understatement or overstatement, respectively. It was a full-time commitment for less than part-time wages, but the most difficult aspect was that every decision I made had a direct impact on someone I knew. When I was dealing with the budget, for example, and needed to eliminate two positions in some office or other, the job almost always belonged to someone I knew down the block or to someone's mother-in-law.

But as tough as it was, it was doubly rewarding. My administration did a lot of positive things to change the city and instill in its residents a real hope for a better future. One of our first initiatives was to attract private investment to expand the tax base and thereby increase our revenues, and to do that we completely changed Peekskill's development policies.

W E'VE ALSO WORKED TO SPUR ECONOMIC DEVELOPMENT ALL over New York State. In every jurisdiction, there are under-developed and underutilized parcels, and these represent enormous untapped revenues for local governments; the key is to find creative ways to tap those resources for the greater good of the community. When I took office as mayor of Peekskill, for example, about 35 percent of the city was tax-exempt. This was in line with a lot of the old inner-city communities in the New York City area, but I was determined to reduce the percentage substantially.

There was a bankrupt boys' school on about seventy-five acres in town, overlooking the Hudson, and I thought the land was a key to our redevelopment efforts. It was a magnificent piece of property, but as it moved toward bankruptcy court it appeared that our only bidders would be a group of Buddhists who wanted to turn the lot into a sanctuary, and a group of Hasidic Jews who hoped to build a synagogue. Either group would have made a fine addition to our diverse community, but neither would have done anything to expand the tax base. The property would have remained tax-exempt, and it was the largest vacant parcel that could have been used to expand the tax base.

I was on the phone constantly, talking to regional developers, hoping to interest them in this piece of land. Whenever I'd read in the paper that one town or other had disapproved someone's development plan, I'd call the developer up and describe our great parcel. "Come to Peekskill," I'd say. "You'll be surprised." I remember talking to one builder in White Plains, and after I outlined our plans for the future he responded that Peekskill was a dying community. When I persisted, he realized that he hadn't made his point. "Peekskill isn't dying," he said, more emphatically. "Peekskill is dead." That was the perception, and too often a perception can become a reality.

But we were persuasive. We put together a package of incentives, trying to find someone to turn the property into private housing units and restore it to Peekskill's tax roles. One local development group showed some interest, and it was joined by a second, from Long Island, the night before the auction. The Long Island developers came into the picture so late that they actually showed up with flashlights to inspect the property.

During the auction, we did what we could to sweeten the package, to keep the developers in the running for the parcel, and in the end a last-minute proposal from Long Island produced the winning bid. I was thrilled. The developers wound up converting the existing buildings to condominiums, and then they built new units on the remaining land. The entire development was an enormous success. We now had over 500 new units of single-family homes on this property, built in a small city with a limited geographic area. The families living there were happy; the developers made money; the city tax base expanded. This was a tremendous boost for the entire region.

I remember driving past the site with Libby and our older kids when the project was nearing completion and feeling a tremendous rush of pride, that we'd given the city a push in the right direction. I thought back to my grandfather, to the hat factory, to his first halting steps on the farm, to the efforts of the Hungarian community to help build the Uriah Hill Elementary School (a school that Emily and Teddy would soon attend), to my father's mail route, to the Pigeon S--- Yacht Club—as we named it—and I could feel the thread of my entire family throughout the fabric of Peekskill. It was a palpable thing. We were still here, and we were making a difference.

I've tried to build on that moment in every office I've held since, to appreciate that in every town there are people whose roots go down as deep as mine in Peekskill, and to take these into account. Over the years, I've given myself many opportunities for such an accounting: I re-upped for a second term as mayor in 1983; in 1984 I ran for the assembly in another race I wasn't supposed to win; and then, in 1992, I finally turned my focus to the senate, in still another race I wasn't meant to win. At each turn, the people could sense that I meant what I said, that I would work as hard as I could to change things, and that I was keenly committed to the community, the region, and the state. They saw it in the way I sought the job, and in the way I did the job. By 1994, when I went up against Mario Cuomo for governor, I'd made a career of facing unbeatable opponents; but I was never afraid that I might not win, and I was proud of the decisions I'd made that had brought me to that place in my life and career. The people saw that, I think, and responded.

Libby and I eventually left Peekskill, in 1993, for a larger house in nearby Garrison, but our roots were still in the Hudson Valley. They still are. We had actually bought the house in Garrison in 1986, but it took awhile to get the magnificent old place in shape, and to get me used to the idea of leaving Peekskill. The joke in the family was that Libby tricked me into Garrison the same way I had tricked her into

Peekskill, but there was really no trickery in either case. It just took a while for each of us to ease into our new situations, for the heart to catch up to the head, and mine were soon enough in alignment. The Garrison house was wonderful—it had been built in 1894 by Governor Hamilton Fish, for his daughter—and as soon as we moved in I knew it was home. This was where we would raise our family. It wasn't Peekskill, but it was close by. I had grown up in a time before suburbanization: We were inside the city limits and yet in the country. But by the time our kids were born, the entire city had been developed; you couldn't even cross Bear Mountain Parkway, let alone play baseball on it, so we went up the road a little way to find the kind of sleepy rural charm we once knew in Peekskill. It was still the Hudson Valley, and it was still home.

Our decision not to live in the governor's mansion in Albany was an easy one for me, and it flowed directly from our love affair with the region and with our adopted home in Garrison. I've received a lot of criticism in Albany for it, as I anticipated, but it doesn't weigh much against the benefits of staying at home. Some people have suggested that I diminish the office by living outside Albany, but I don't see it that way. Indeed, if I had asked Libby and the kids to leave home, they'd have rightly seen it as a diminution of the family. Being governor is important, and I am dedicated to doing the best possible job for the people of New York State. But being a father is more important. There will always be another governor, but for my kids there'll never be another father, another childhood, another home. On issues as basic as where I choose to live, my commitment to my family must override my commitment to the state. What kind of person would I be if it didn't? I don't mean to suggest that any of my predecessors who chose to live in Albany in some way shortchanged their families by doing so. Not at all. It's just that for us, the Hudson Valley is home, and we were at a time in our lives when it would have been selfish of me to uproot everyone.

As it is, our kids face enough challenges. They've done well with the transition from being the anonymous children of a state assemblyman and senator to being the somewhat prominent children of the governor, largely because they've stayed put. They go to the same schools; they have the same friends; they play on the same teams. But it isn't all smooth. Teddy, at fourteen, told me he didn't like having to wear his last name on his hockey jersey; when his team played in another town and one of the opposing players asked him if he was related to the governor, he would say I was his uncle. He was smart enough to know there weren't that many Patakis around, and that no one would have believed him if he denied the connection entirely; but he shouldn't have had to think things through in that way, at that age. He shouldn't have had to ask me to make sure the state troopers on my security detail didn't show up at his lacrosse games wearing suits, walkie-talkies, and earphones. He didn't necessarily mind the fact that they were there (he actually liked it when they cheered him on), but he didn't like the way they stood out. He just wanted to be an ordinary kid.

That's the hardest part of my being governor, the impact it's had on my children. It's stripped them of their ordinariness, changed the stakes a little bit, put them into a spotlight they didn't seek for themselves. They're good kids, but there's enough going on in their lives without having an extra layer of particulars to deal with.

There are so many obstacles facing parents today that it's a wonder our children don't implode from our anxiety. I understand the constraints placed on two-income families, the way parents and kids must budget their time together in order to come out whole; I understand the shifting family dynamics that permeate not only our inner cities but the heartland as well; I understand that too often, in our effort to protect our children, we program them in such a way that there's no time for them to relax, hang out, or do nothing at all; and I understand that in the onslaught of images and sound that reach our kids through television and the various strains of popular culture, it is sometimes difficult to find acceptable role models and patterns of behavior.

By comparison I had it easy as a kid. I didn't have to deal with things like drugs, sex, or gang violence; in our group no one used drugs, no one had sex, and no one beat the tar out of someone else for no apparent reason. I pretty much skipped the drug culture—or, I should say, it skipped me. Recreational drugs weren't prominent when I was at Yale; I drank a lot of beer, but no one I knew was smoking dope, taking pills, or dropping acid. That would come later, at Columbia. By the time I was in law school, almost everyone was willing to experiment; but I never really had any interest in drugs. In my crowd the routine was to go down to the Gold Rail every night, drink beer, and kick around the social issues of the day.

In my own case, it wasn't until my last year in law school that I finally tried marijuana. I was with a couple of good friends, and we cooked some of the stuff in a can of baked beans. None of us were smokers, and we'd heard that this was a good method. A lot of people baked marijuana into brownies, but we didn't have the wherewithal for that kind of cooking, so we just sprinkled some of it over a can of warmed-up beans and dug in.

If that was all it was, I could safely say that I, too, never inhaled; but I did smoke pot the conventional way a few times after that, and, yes, I did inhale. But marijuana never had any real appeal for me. I liked drinking beer because I liked the taste, especially when I was dehydrated after a couple of hours of basketball or touch football. I loved the social interaction. We'd sit around a pitcher of beer and solve the world's problems. Most of my friends who smoked marijuana tended to just go off in their own heads somewhere, and underneath it there seemed to be a desire to lose control and tune out. It was too antisocial for me. I'd rather shoot the bull and have a few laughs than lose myself in irrational thought.

But I was fortunate. I had a chance to develop physically and emotionally in high school without the pressures of drugs. High school is a time of enormous growth and enormous stress. You have tough exams. You have tough social situations. I've seen what Emily has gone through and what Teddy is about to face. You have a tough time figuring out who you are and where you fit in the spectrum of things. To have to go through all this with drugs and alcohol as a false escape hatch is a sad and dangerous development.

It is terrifying to me—both as a parent and as an elected official— that drugs have reached even into our elementary schools. The average age of first experimentation is now under thirteen, and that's just the average; clearly, there are ten- and eleven-year-olds doing some of that experimenting. In some communities, drugs get kids even younger. I look at the statistics, and then I think of Allison and Owen and their friends, and I cringe. In this respect, I'm appalled by what we've allowed our world to become. One of the reasons it's so hard to send the right message to our children on a personal level is that, nationally, the message no longer flows from the top. It was easy to make fun of Nancy Reagan's "Just Say No!" campaign, but the fact remains that teenage drug use was declining during the Reagan administration, and it's been rising since.

Let's face it: If we don't get a strong, consistent message from the White House, or from our image makers and tastemakers in Hollywood and on Madison Avenue, we have to make sure to convey the message at the state level. In New York, we have some good proactive programs designed to educate and enlighten children. It's never too early to start. Owen, our own youngest, came home from school with antidrug messages when he was six or seven, and he shared them with his brother and sisters over the dinner table; and I think those bulletins resonated with the older kids because they flowed through their little brother.

Of course, Libby and I don't rely on Owen to do our parenting. We talk to our kids about drugs and about anything else that touches their lives. As a parent, you have to be on top of everything. Or at least try to be. The only "magic" in setting children on the right path is being there for them—at all times and at all costs—and following the right path yourself. Since becoming governor, I've missed out on a lot: school plays, recitals, basketball games, and even some birthday parties. But I've tried to always be there for the nuts and bolts. I probably spend more time traveling across New York State than any governor in a long time, and I'll travel to any remote corner for the slightest reason, but I try to be home as much as I can. I'm there to help them understand the difference between right and wrong; to sort through the influences from television, movies, and professional sports; and to identify appropriate role models.

Finding role models is an area too many parents ignore, but even if we paid special attention to this, I'm not sure how much it would help. There are precious few role models out there—too few people deserving of our kids' emulation. When I was a kid, there were real heroes in the world of sports, for instance; but there seems to be a real lack of sportsmanship among today's athletes, and it results from the in-your-face antics of too many of our top stars. Contrast the strutting of some of today's basketball and football players with more gentlemanly, team-oriented athletes like Pelé, an international superstar just before my oldest child was born, and you see how empty we are in this area.

I once saw Pelé score a goal, when he was playing for the New York Cosmos, and his instinct was to jump, wave, and throw his arms into the air. But he caught himself and went over to the other team's goalie to apologize. Then he ran to the other side of the field before jumping up and hugging his own teammates. His immediate joy at having scored a goal was overcome by his respect for his opponents. As much as he wanted to celebrate, he couldn't show up the other team.

Few people play like Pelé anymore, but fortunately, my children grew up with an exception in their midst. Elton Brand was one of the most intensely recruited high school basketball players in the country, although what most people outside Peekskill didn't realize was that he was also a terrific kid. He led the high school basketball team to two state championships his last three years in school. He played Santa Claus to Emily's Mrs. Santa Claus in the first-grade play at Uriah Hill and stood as a fine archetype to my entire family. We watched him play throughout his growing up and took special pride in knowing him. That he was being raised by a single mother in the same housing project my cousins grew up in was significant, but not as meaningful as his unselfish style of play or his manner off the court. I never once saw him show off, in an era when showing off was the custom of the game and the neighborhood. He wound up getting 90's on his exams in school, achieving 1,200 on his college boards, and enrolling at Duke, and we're looking forward to rooting for him at the college level; but mostly what we're rooting for is that he will hold on to his values and remember where he came from.

Every community should be graced with an Elton Brand, to hold up to its children, because we've reached a point where we need a positive to counter every negative. But unfortunately there's too much chest-thumping bravado in too many of our school yards, and it extends throughout the world of sports. It's all show, and it's an unhealthy show. It's troubling. It tells the world we don't care about the other person, that competition is no longer a game but an act of gamesmanship. Sport should be not just a test of strength and skill, but also a test of teamwork and character. I want to instill in my children the kind of self-confidence that allows them to believe in themselves without having to beat that belief into anyone else. But it's a hard sell when a star baseball player spits in the face of an umpire or an opponent, or when one of the best guards in basketball puts his coach in a choke hold and threatens to kill him.

There's a growing tolerance of intolerable behavior. It's a fundamental problem. Many of the problems we face in our schools can be traced to the slow acceptance of what was once unacceptable. This makes it difficult for our kids to learn, because they keep seeing the lines redrawn. "The line is no longer here, it's back there." "That used to be the rule, but now it's okay to do it this other way." These changes happen by degrees, and we allow them to happen also by degrees.

There was a good story recently from Tuckahoe, in Westchester County, that shows us the kind of message we should be sending our children. Tuckahoe's high school football team was in the third quarter of a tight game. Two of its players were ejected for unsportsmanlike conduct, and a few of their teammates threw their helmets on the field in disgust at the referee's ruling. The coach, upset not by the referee but by his own players' reaction, pulled the entire team off the field and forfeited the game. I thought this sent exactly the right message. It wasn't a popular message, but it was the right one. It wasn't "Win at all costs." It was "Play by the rules; respect those who enforce the rules and those who play against you; or don't play at all."

These are the lessons we must impart to our children, and Libby and I find them where we can, throughout the Hudson Valley. The lessons for our children are in the land, in our values, and in the good people of our community. We're not perfect, far from it, but then no one is. And yet those values of work, respect, and courtesy are all around us. They are in our history. It doesn't matter to our kids that their father is the governor of the state of New York, or that their mother is the first lady, and it shouldn't. What matters is that we've built our lives by trying to do what's right—for our community, for our families, and for ourselves.

I collect stories from my law school friends and my Yale roommates, and on some levels it seems I haven't accomplished what they have: they've lived all over the world, worked on all kinds of important deals, helped to shape policy and advance major projects; they make salaries in the high six or seven figures.

But then I look within and see that I've accomplished more than I'd ever dreamed—and certainly more than most. It's easy to put in perspective when I think of how many apples I'd have to sell to earn a governor's salary, how many letters I'd have to deliver. How can you put a value on taking your daughter to dinner at the White House, or getting to introduce your family to the Pope? The experience has been truly wonderful. As a child, I had everything money *couldn't* buy, and because of that I had it better than most. I may have moved only a few miles from the house I grew up in, but I've done more than I ever dreamed. I've worked to make a difference in the lives of the people around me; I've built a big, loving family with a woman who shares my hopes and my heart; and I've helped to sustain the Pataki line that runs through the hard soil of the Hudson Highlands.

We've allowed the farm to fall into disrepair in recent years, but I still have dreams that someday we'll get the stand up and running again. My father's gone, and my grandparents are gone, and my mother now lives in the Garrison house with us; my cousins are scattered all across the country. Life has taken most of us someplace else. All that's left of how it was for me as a kid is the farm itself, and even that's been diluted by time and circumstances. Right now, the land is probably worth more to a developer than it could yield in a hundred years of crops.

But a part of the orchards are still there, and one of our best fields is still there. Some of Grandpa's old equipment is lying around, and the stand itself remains, though it needs a new roof. The corncrib, the wagon, the apple trees . . . they're all waiting to be restored to what they were. Libby is willing, and so are the kids, and I'm sure we could lure a few cousins back to help out. Why not? We'll plant our corn, tend our trees, and maybe get the grapes trimmed back and growing again. We'll light a wood fire and bring back the aunts and uncles— those who are still around—and all the other cousins, with their kids, and in some cases their grandkids, and serve up a good old-fashioned Hungarian bacon roast. And we'll get back to planting our tomatoes six or seven weeks ahead of everyone else, just as my father and grandfather always did, because one year, I'm sure of it, they'll make it through a spring without frost. And that would be something.

10

November 8, 1994—
7:00 P.M.

W E LEFT THE LONG ISLAND RAIL ROAD PLATFORMS AS THE
rush hour began to fade, and my spirit began to soar. I was
buoyed by the surge of good feeling I felt from the people, but finally
realized there was nothing more to do but wait for what would come
next. I'd shaken every hand there was to shake. My message was out
there, and the message coming back to me was that it had taken. The
people wanted change.

We crept through crosstown traffic from Penn Station beneath the
blare of WCBS radio, whose announcers told us that Senator Frank
Lautenberg was winning in New Jersey by three points and Mario
Cuomo was carrying New York by two.

"Turn that off," I told Keegan, up in the driver's seat. I didn't need
to hear all this talk about exit polls, but more than that I didn't accept
it. We'd been getting a great response, all across the state. "We're going
to win," I said, to myself as much as to anyone else. "I don't care what
those reports say."

"I'm sure of it," Keegan shouted back.

"You really think so, Dad?" Teddy asked. "You really think you're
going to win?"

I pride myself on being able to honestly judge a crowd's reaction to me and my ideas. It's not an easy thing—to hear not just only the positives but also the negatives when you're out in public fourteen or sixteen hours a day—but over the years my own take on people had proved a fairly accurate measure. Here, in just the past week, I'd seen a huge difference in the crowds: people were more enthusiastic, more positive, more optimistic. And on this night, down by those trains, the response was sensational.

"Yeah, Teddy," I said, "I really do." And I did.

Teddy said he hoped I was right. Doherty, still thinking of the WCBS report, said nothing. We snaked through traffic to the Hilton, to drop Teddy off to join his brother and sisters and the rest of the family in our campaign suite. Doherty and I went to meet Carll Tucker, Bill Plunkett, Brad Race, and Virgil Conway—some of my "kitchen cabinet"—for a drink at Ben Bensen's steak house, where my four great friends, who had helped me through the ups and downs of the campaign, had planned what they hoped would be a celebratory dinner.

I couldn't stay. Doherty and I were headed to meet Libby, Senator D'Amato, Charlie Gargano, John O'Mara, and Arthur Finkelstein for what was to have been an intimate dinner at a small northern Italian restaurant on East 50th Street. The restaurant had been chosen for luck: D'Amato and company had eaten there on election night in 1992, when the polls had him losing to Bob Abrams by a double-digit margin and he proved them wrong and won. We were hoping some of that good fortune would find us, so we even made a point of sitting at the same table.

I walked down the steps into the restaurant, about ten feet below street level, and was ushered to a back corner table.

"Governor!" D'Amato yelled, with his customary exuberance. He stood to greet me.

"Don't call me that," I shot back in a friendly way. "You know I think it's bad luck."

"All right," he said, "I'll hold off for now, but in three hours . . ." His voice trailed off. He knew he didn't have to finish his sentence for me to get his meaning. I walked around the table, collecting hugs and handshakes. Libby gave me a big kiss. The mood of our small party was upbeat and happy. That is, everyone was upbeat and happy except Arthur Finkelstein.

"You hear anything more on the exit polls?" Arthur asked Doherty, who had come in behind me.

"Exit polls!" Alfonse laughed. "Who listens to exit polls? They had me down by six, and look what happened. And besides, I met this little old Italian lady at the supermarket in Island Park this afternoon. She said she voted for that George guy. She said her whole family is voting for that George guy."

Alfonse was convinced. I was carrying Island Park, and so I was destined to carry the state.

O'Mara chimed in, "They're coming out of the woods to vote upstate. I tell you, in Chemung County and across the Southern Tier we are going to shatter every record with today's vote."

Arthur wasn't so sure. "That's nice," he said, "but has anyone heard any numbers?" Arthur was a numbers man—in my view, the best numbers man. To him an election was all about making the case on the issues and then looking at the numbers; either they were there or they weren't.

"CBS radio still has us down two," Doherty replied.

Arthur turned pale. He stood up and began pacing. "I can't understand it," he said. "I have us winning by four. How can we be losing?"

My confidence, my ability to "feel" the crowd, my belief in the momentum carrying us to victory . . . all of it began to drain from me as fast as the color from Arthur's face. It was there, and then it was gone. I'd only been at the restaurant a few minutes, and already I'd heard enough. I wanted to ignore the exit polls and call back the good feeling I'd had at Penn Station just a few moments before.

"You know how it is, Arthur," I said. "They say that the Democrats vote earlier. Seniors vote earlier. The cities vote earlier than the rural areas. The suburban workers and commuters always vote last. That's just how it is. Of course I'm going to be a couple of points behind at this point."

Arthur Finkelstein was the last person I needed to be telling this. "Don't talk to me about exit polls," he said. "I worked with the networks on how to do their exit polls twenty years ago. They know how to factor in time of day. They know how to factor in geography and demographics. They know about momentum. If they say we're two points behind, we're probably two points behind."

"You're all forgetting the little old lady in Island Park," D'Amato quipped.

I lost my appetite. So did almost everyone else at the table. Still, I couldn't help thinking that Arthur was reading too much into too little or not enough into far too much. Just then, Tom Doherty burst back into the restaurant with the latest bulletin: Chuck Haytaian, the speaker of the New Jersey assembly who was making a grab for Lautenberg's U.S. Senate seat, had apparently overcome his three-point shortfall in his own four o'clock exit polling with a final-hour rush at the polls. The race—again, according to WCBS—was now too close to call.

This was great news. The New Jersey polls closed at eight o'clock, one hour earlier than those in New York, and if the race was too close to call, the WCBS exit poll showing him down by three percentage points had to be wrong. "Thank God," Arthur sighed, thinking that perhaps the news organization had the wrong systems in place for its late-afternoon polling. We all breathed a little easier. Libby and Alfonse actually sat down at the table and went back to eating, and I remember thinking what a shame it would be to let all this good food go to waste because of a little anxiety.

Doherty went back out to the Suburban to work the phones and listen to the radio. He returned just a beat or two later, quietly this time. "Well, it's over in New Jersey," he said somberly. "Lautenberg's won."

"By how much?" Arthur wanted to know.

"Three points."

By now, Arthur was an emotional wreck. He was distressed by the exit polls, and then reassured by Haytaian's apparent surge, and then distressed all over again—and to see him distressed was itself distressing. Throughout the campaign, Arthur had been our rock, a steady voice of optimism; even when public polls had us down twenty points, he was sure we were going to win. The cold, unemotional reputation of most political consultants did not fit Arthur Finkelstein. He was no hired gun. He really wanted to win. He cared. He cared so much that he stood and walked out of the restaurant.

"Don't forget the Italian lady," D'Amato called after him.

Arthur didn't hear him. The restaurant was below street level, so he walked up the outside steps to the sidewalk, and I could see his feet through the high windows of the restaurant. He was pacing back and forth, back and forth, like a frantic Jackie Gleason in a *Honeymooners* skit. My optimism ebbed with every step. Maybe Arthur was right, I thought, my eyes following his shoes up and down the street. Maybe there was something to worry about.

I looked around the table and could see I wasn't alone in my second thoughts. Even Al D'Amato was starting to doubt his Island Park lady. Maybe she wasn't an omen at all.

I couldn't stay there and watch all these people unravel on me. Win or lose, it wasn't the way I wanted to spend election night, so Libby and I excused ourselves and made our way out to the Suburban. By this point, I was certain I would lose—well, maybe not certain, but at least willing to concede the point. Ed Keegan, himself a steadying force of unwavering optimism, was in his own version of panic in the front of the car. He'd been taking me around the state since before I even announced my candidacy, and for the first time he started to fall apart on me too. He had a phone to each ear, desperate for some last-minute piece of positive news, and he had the radio tuned to the all-news station, and he was suddenly beside himself with worry. "We're going to lose," he kept saying, almost in a chant. "We're going to lose. I just know it."

"Have a little faith, Eddie," I said, trying to muster some of my own.

Doherty was in the car with us, in the front passenger seat, but he wasn't saying anything. He just hung on yet another phone, waiting for information and looking depressed. He actually had his head in his hands, in such a way that I finally realized what the expression "head

in hand" really meant. I turned to Libby in the backseat alongside me
and took her hand. She was holding up pretty well, so I tried to ignore
the two overwrought men in the front and focus on Libby's more positive demeanor; but no matter how I dressed things up in my head it
was still a depressing picture all around, and I started to think that
maybe the governor's office wasn't in the cards. Maybe this wasn't my
year.

"George," Libby said, sensing my unease, "we're going to win. We
have to win. The state needs you."

"Thanks, Lib," I said. "We'll know soon enough."

I worried about the future—not my own, mind you, but the future
of all New Yorkers. I worried what the state would look like after four
more years of Mario Cuomo.

Losing the chance to really change things, to make a fundamental
difference in the lives of millions of New Yorkers, to give my kids the
same confidence in their future as I had in mine when I was growing
up in Peekskill . . . these were the things that mattered most. Losing
wouldn't kill me. The world would still spin on its axis, and I'd still
have my family, my health, and my prospects. Before getting into the
campaign, I had thought through what I would do if I lost the race, so
that I'd be pleasantly surprised in victory as opposed to crushed in defeat. So this wasn't entirely new ground to me; it's just that I never expected to be treading over it again after feeling so confident over the
past few months, and especially after the way things had gone in Penn
Station just a few hours earlier.

It would have been easy to sit there in the car thinking that, in defeat, my campaign would have accomplished nothing, but I didn't believe that. It meant everything that I had tried, that I hadn't stayed on
the fringes and accepted the status quo, that I at least would no longer
be an accessory to the policies of Mario Cuomo that were destroying
the state.

And then something strange happened, on the drive back to the
Hilton. With Arthur and his back-and-forth pacing no longer an issue,
I started to think that we had a good chance. I was back again in the

mood of those train platforms, of the crowds I'd been with over the past week. I once more had the sense I was able to pick up every time I stepped out on the street, the steadfast conviction that Mario Cuomo was the wrong man to lead the state for the next four years and that people were bound to recognize that. I decided to trust my gut and ignore the numbers; and as we pulled into the drop-off area at the Hilton, my faith returned. It didn't take much to get me going, one way or the other, but here I was feeling good—right along with Libby— about our chances, and what we might soon accomplish.

There were perhaps thirty or forty people waiting for us up in the suite. My mother. My brother, Lou. The kids. Friends. Extended family. Annie O'Sullivan, my right hand, who'd been with me since my very first run for the assembly. Alfonse, Arthur, O'Mara, and Charlie pulled in from the restaurant. Rick Garvey had come in from Chicago, Mac Hansing from Ohio. Cousin Bobby was there from Michigan, and Cousin Judy from Rochester. Some of my close friends later told me they came expecting me to lose and to have to bolster me in defeat, but it was nice to have them there just the same. The television was already on in the main sitting room, and I grabbed the remote control from one of the kids. I had the most at stake, I thought, so I might as well have the power to change the channels. I flipped from station to station, looking for partial returns. These partial returns were mostly meaningless—like a third-quarter basketball score—but I wanted to know what was going on, even in bits and pieces.

What really mattered, though, were the calls that kept coming in from around the state. We had some of our key people posted at election boards in targeted counties, and they started checking in about a half hour or so ahead of the reports we were getting from the local news organizations. Tim Carey manned the phones to upstate, and Mike Finnegan for the New York City suburbs. There had been a record turnout upstate, which was what we were hoping for, and the early returns from places like Orange County were extremely encouraging. Indeed, I soon learned, we took Orange County in a landslide, but then that good news was countered with news of our historic drubbing in New York City.

The calls had us winning big upstate, but not big enough in the metropolitan area. We had a great result in Suffolk and a terrible result in Nassau. We had that great result in Orange, and then a disappointing tally in Westchester. And all along we were getting killed in New York City, to such an extent that I wasn't sure our margins elsewhere would be enough to get the job done for us. We were running the lowest city vote totals of any successful candidate in the history of the state, so to assume a win was more than a little presumptuous.

All of a sudden, the television coverage shifted. It was almost as if we'd all willed it to happen. After forty-five minutes of Cuomo's being ahead by two or three points, the results started to become favorable. I began to inch ahead, as reports came in from our rural upstate counties. Then a call came in from the Erie County Republican boss, Tom Reynolds, and my world was forever changed.

"Governor!" Reynolds screamed into the phone.

Here was that "governor" nonsense again. "Don't call me that, Tommy," I said. "You know I'm superstitious. How's it going?"

"Governor!" he screamed again, louder this time. No one can yell louder than Tom Reynolds, and from the roar in the background I could tell that our Erie County headquarters was packed, and charged. "You carried Erie by 30,000 votes," he screamed, louder still.

My eardrums rattled and my heart thumped. I couldn't think what to say.

"Did you hear me, Governor? Over 30,000 votes!" The headquarters crowd seemed to cheer more forcefully each time the "boss" announced the total. "You're the governor!" he finally screamed. "Can you believe it? You're the governor."

"Tommy," I quietly asked, "can you repeat that please?"

"You're the governor!" he repeated. I swear, he was so loud I might have heard him without the phone.

"No, not that part," I said. "The vote. Tell me the totals again."

"You carried Erie County by over 30,000," he repeated.

And at that point I knew. Before that moment, I had thought I would win, I had felt I would win, but now I knew. I knew what it meant to carry Erie County. The city of Buffalo is in Erie County. There are more than 1 million people in Erie County, most of them blue-collar Democrats, and no Republican ever carries it. Rockefeller never carried it. D'Amato never carried it. And I hadn't just limped in, according to Reynolds's account; I had carried it by more than I carried Westchester, Rockland, and Putnam counties combined. This meant that something tremendous was happening out there, and we were in the thick of it. The record turnout, and our record margins in some traditionally Democratic upstate strongholds, would be more than enough to nullify Cuomo's landslide in the city itself.

Looking back, I think the best thing about this moment—and it really was just a moment—was that I was the only one who knew. I mean this quite literally. For a beat or two, I was the only person in the entire state of New York who could say for certain who had won the race. Not who "was winning" the race, not who "would probably win" the race, but who had actually won. Tom Reynolds and the crew up in Erie, for all their wild enthusiasm, didn't have the rest of the picture; and the rest of the picture—Arthur, Kieran, Libby, the people on the local news desks—didn't yet have the numbers from Erie. For the time being, it all flowed through me, and I took that one moment and held it close. It was a great feeling. The campaign suite was all chaos and commotion, with everyone's *not* knowing, and this last piece would surely raise the mood of the room through the ceiling. I wanted to stretch this moment out, savor it, and remember it for what it was. I was alone in my knowing, surrounded by the people who knew me best and wanted only the best for me.

I hung up the phone and found Libby. "Lib," I said, "I'm going to be the governor."

"Who was that?" she asked, indicating the telephone. She knew me well enough not to simply accept my conclusions; others did that; she wanted the facts.

"Tom Reynolds, up in Buffalo. Said we carried Erie County by 30,000 votes. We can't lose."

We hugged. She knew. Soon everyone would know. I turned to my friends standing next to me and told them about Erie. They were thrilled but didn't quite know what it meant. They didn't understand the numbers, or the history, and I was too caught up in it to explain. The professionals knew. The strategists among us quickly sniffed out what was going on, and their knowing mixed with mine, and soon the room was roaring with excitement. My one short moment of knowing had mushroomed into almost everyone else's. The kids were cheering and yelling as if they were at a ball game, my mother was beaming, and Libby stood by my side and helped me soak it all in.

We turned back to the television, and in about ten minutes found confirmation on Channel 2: "CBS is now able to project that Republican George Pataki will defeat Mario Cuomo and become the next governor of New York."

The place went mad. Cheers. Hugs. Toasts. Tears. All the emotions that come from a great victory in a historic battle against great odds. At least, we all thought it was a great victory in a historic battle against great odds. Perspective is everything.

I pointed the remote back to the television and found another station declaring me the next governor. Now I wasn't the only one who knew, and it wasn't just the rest of us here in this room, and it wasn't just those New Yorkers watching Channel 2; it was everyone; it was out there, done, and about to happen.

We were all swept up by it, right away. My mind raced over everything else that might happen in the next few moments. I looked over to the single telephone we had set up on one side of the room—an open line to Mario Cuomo's headquarters, the receiver held down with masking tape and a hand-lettered "Do Not Touch" sign fixed to the base—and wondered when it might ring. This was one of the details I'd actually stopped to think through; it was a small courtesy, but I wanted to keep the line clear, to make sure the governor didn't have to wait if he wanted to call and offer his concession, or his congratulations, or whatever. I knew that if the situation had been reversed (and the nail-biting of the previous few hours had me thinking it very nearly was), I would have hated to hear a busy signal at the other end when I surrendered. It's tough enough to reach out to your opponent after a tense campaign, without being kept waiting.

As it turned out, we were putting too fine a point on things with

our consideration. Mario Cuomo never called that night. We kept a
staff person by the phone, but it never rang.

It was just as well. I'm not sure I would have known what to say if
he had called. The campaign had turned rancorous in the final weeks,
and it would have been nearly impossible to pretend there were no
hard feelings. I didn't even know what to say to the press or to the
other friends and supporters (thousands of them) gathered in the ballroom downstairs.

For weeks, people had been suggesting I prepare a victory speech,
just in case, but that, to me, was far worse than being called governor. I
wasn't one to tempt fate, and it dawned on me now that the nation
would be watching when I went downstairs to make my remarks. This
was big news: Mario Cuomo, a fixture on the national political scene
for more than a decade, potential president, denied a fourth term as
governor. And the cameras would be looking at me as the man who
did the denying. In the eyes of the media, I'd gone from a regional
hopeful to a nationally prominent elected official in the space of a
heartbeat, and I realized that in order to hit the ground running I
needed to make a strong first impression.

There was a whole inventory of words running through my head,
but I didn't want to reach back and rehash an old speech. That wasn't
what this moment deserved. I wanted to be fresh, spontaneous, and
open. I wanted to tell the people what this moment meant to me and
my family, and what it might mean to them in the four years ahead. I
wanted to be sure to thank everyone who had worked so tirelessly
during the long months of the campaign. I wanted to get it right.

A group of us piled into the elevator and rode downstairs to face
our future. I'd learned early on that being sincere meant more than being glib, and after all this, how could I be anything but sincere?

Tom Doherty remembers that there was not enough room in the
elevator cab for all of us, and he had to race down about forty floors to
beat us to the podium. The rest of the people in the elevator remember
the short ride down as a brief pocket of quiet in the middle of the
frenzy. Their world would change dramatically in the months ahead,

and the changes would hit them full in the face when the elevator doors opened and spilled us out into the ballroom to face the crowd.

For them, that elevator ride was the sweet pause I had known on the phone to Erie County, the calm before the storm. For me, it was a couple of minutes more to think out what I would say. I thought about the path I'd chosen, the decisions I'd made that had brought me to this place. I thought about my father, up at the firemen's home, and wondered if any of this was registering for him. I thought of our kids, not knowing if they could finish the year in school or if we would have to pull them out and reestablish them in Albany after all. I thought of my cousins, and our lifelong friends and neighbors, many of whom had traveled clear across the country to be with us on this night. I thought of my tireless supporters, who believed in me and what we might accomplish. But mostly I thought about the farm, and about how I was raised, and the values my parents and grandparents had instilled in me. I thought about how it was, and how it could be again.

11

Against the Tide

WHEN I WAS A KID, MY AUNT ZELMA USED TO PACK A BUNCH of us cousins into the car and head out for Jones Beach. Once or twice each summer, this was our great treat, a great memory. Aunt Zelma was the only woman in the family who drove at that time, this was the only time we got to see the ocean, and we all looked forward to the outing as if it were Christmas.

One of our cherished rituals, on those long summer days at the shore, was to build a string of giant sand forts along the water's edge, sit ourselves down in them, and wait. We made a contest out of it, to see whose walls would stand the longest as the waves started to come in. The challenge was to start at the same baseline—usually, a couple of feet in from the most recent high-water mark—and then to see who withstood the eventual onslaught of the waves the longest. Of course, none of us could beat the tides, and we'd then have a mad scramble to shore up our efforts where we were weak, to beat the next rush of surf, to do what we could to patch, repair, and rethink. We would rebuild the walls whenever the tide knocked them down, but eventually we'd all get wiped out.

I played the same game throughout my growing up, even in law school when I rented a beach house with friends, and I do it now with my own kids. We're always digging, building, and strategizing to see which one of us can hold out longest, but ultimately the tide always wins. It's no contest, so the game becomes a test against each other. Over the years, we've tried different schemes: high walls of hard sand, deep moats to absorb the first waves, a gradual trench to divert the current.

However it plays out, it's always tremendous fun, and a great way to pass the time between high tides; but I've often wondered, is what we politicians do pretty much the same thing? Are we just trying to hold back the tide, working against the "inevitable" forces of our economic and political system? Can you really make a city like Peekskill—a turn-of-the-century factory town—into a city of the twenty-first century? Can you turn a northeastern state like New York away from its "inevitable" decline and back again to greatness? Are you really making a difference, or are you back on the beach, sitting in your crude little forts, as the shadows grow longer and you wait to be washed over by time and tide. At the end of the day, will anyone even know you were there?

That might be politics, I've often feared, and wouldn't that be a shame. Or, at least, that could be government, or how government might act if we bend to the inevitability. You see and hear it all the time, even under the most benign of circumstances. "You're all alike," they'll say. Or, "nothing will change," or, "I don't care."

As I moved forward in state government, there were times when it seemed that all I was doing was simply forestalling the fated tide of decline. Despite our best efforts in the assembly, taxes would rise, inevitably. Jobs would leave for the South, inevitably. The public interest would shift; logic would step aside to make way for expedience. This feeling of powerlessness against the inevitable was never more apparent than during the strange dance of state budget negotiations, an accident of government totally foreign to the kind of commonsense problem-solving I was used to on the farm. And it was never more frustrating than in 1990, when I was still in the assembly—and very much in the minority. Cuomo's budget, we knew, while raising taxes, would result in a deficit that year (an election year), and yet nobody would talk about it. We could vote against it, as we had in the past, but voting against it wasn't enough. We had to get people talking about how destructive it was for the future of the state. We had to let the people know that poor choices were being made in Albany. We must not just vote no, but actually change things, make a real difference.

A group of us assembly Republicans determined to filibuster the budget. Another group of us would crisscross the state to interest local reporters in the story. This was our strategy against the coming tide. The press in Albany generally ignored us, so we took our case to the people back home, and in the meantime we took turns keeping the debate on the floor—asking each other questions, holding forth on this and that. It was the only means at our disposal to stop time, as it were, to make sure we were heard.

It was actually fun to filibuster, to finally not just sit on the sidelines voting no, even as it was somewhat troubling to have to do so. In a sense, it was like a game—holding back the tide—but a game I thought was keenly important. And we were winning! For the first time in my assembly career, we had the majority confounded. They didn't know what to do to reclaim the floor. We were working within the law (or, at least, within the established rules of debate), and all they could do was wait us out. And wait. And wait.

Finally, at about three o'clock in the morning, when all the Albany reporters had left for the night, the assembly Democratic leader decided that they would suspend the rules of debate and move to a vote. It was an absolute abrogation of procedure, but the leaders no doubt thought that because of the lateness of the hour and absence of reporters they could get away with it. What an outrage! A Republican assemblyman who was sitting next to me shared my indignation, but he showed his displeasure in a rather unusual way. He stood, stuck out his right arm, palm down, and shouted, "Heil, Hitler!"

It was an outrageous and irresponsible display. While it was meant to suggest that the Democratic leadership was resorting to totalitarian tactics in illegally suspending the rules, it raised all the wrong images, and set off a swirl of contention. The filibuster was over—lost in the ruckus—and the budget passed without further debate or incident, despite the "no" votes of the minority Republicans.

It was a maddening session (perhaps my most difficult day in the legislature), and I came away frustrated not only at our ineffectiveness but also at having taken part. When you're in the middle of something you know is wrong, it's enormously disheartening to be powerless. Ultimately, you're a participant, the same as anyone else. And this wasn't even a legitimate discourse on democracy. It wasn't just a disagreement on policy. It was a bipartisan agreement to enact a budget that put the interests of government—more accurately those of politicians and their careers—ahead of the interests and needs of the people of New York. It was a fraud on the people, enacted to protect the incumbents, including Republicans in the senate who were willing to look the other way in order to return Mario Cuomo and company to office. It was a question of deliberately deceiving the public—indeed, just a few weeks after the 1990 election the extent of that deception was finally revealed: The Cuomo budget carried a $6 billion deficit, far worse than any of us had anticipated. The legislature was called back. Taxes were raised even more. School aid was cut in the middle of the fiscal year. Aid to local and county governments was slashed. All kinds of tough decisions were made that resulted in suffering which wouldn't have had to happen if the process had only had some integrity. And I came away thinking I was in the wrong line of work. For all my effort as an elected official, I was right back again on Jones Beach, doing what I could to shore up our sand walls but ultimately succumbing to the tides, to forces beyond my control. At the end of the day, the budget looked no different for my having tried to help shape it.

The assembly wasn't the only place I was occasionally made to feel unable to hold back the destructive tides of government. My very first month in the senate, after having unseated a long-standing incumbent content to go along with the status quo, I got another taste of how things were, and how they would probably be for the time being.

While many of my new colleagues kept telling me in private, "Stick to your guns," they publicly allowed the senate majority leader, Ralph Marino, to run the senate as if he were a junior partner in the Cuomo administration. New York was going downhill, and while assembly Democrats were full partners, the Republican majority were silent partners in its rapid decline. The senate leadership was too content to be bought off with appropriations, large staff allotments, and Cuomo's tacit agreement not to campaign against them to provide any real opposition. They were satisfied to achieve a minor course correction in New York's long decline, so long as that course correction didn't rock the boat.

From my perspective, though, I knew that if we didn't rock the boat—and hard!—it was going to sink. (You'll have to forgive all these maritime metaphors, but they go back to my original point.) I grew up believing that if you choose to seek public office, you have an obligation to the people who elect you to that office to do absolutely everything in your power to make the most of it, not just to work for your reelection. An elective office is not an entitlement. It's not ceremonial. It's not meant to be a permanent way of life. You're the only one. You're the only mayor of the town, the only senator from the district, the only governor of the state, and you have a moral contract to use every ounce of your energy and ability to try to achieve what you think is right for the people.

It was quickly apparent that I'd infiltrated a closed fraternity in the senate. I'd known this, but I'd never come up against it in such conspicuous terms. In New York an overwhelming majority of all state legislators are reelected, a fact which suggests that our government is not entirely open to new ideas and outside opinions. It is harder to lose an election to the New York legislature than it was to be removed from the old Soviet Politburo, and in my time I realized that once you were in, you could get by with little effort and initiative. For too many people, the job became a birthright.

As a state senator, I set out to do something about the senate leadership's failure to stand up to Cuomo, and ran into a wall. The budget for 1993 was handed down for our approval, and we were expected to get behind it without any substantive negotiations or deliberations. Again, this was outrageous, but that's how things were done. Cuomo's budgets increased spending each year by an average of nearly *three times* the rate of inflation—not one year but every year. The numbers were unconscionable, and yet they were ratified with hardly any debate at all, and in 1993 I was about to see it firsthand.

My first senate budget conference, held as usual on the third floor of the Capitol, down the hall from the senate chambers, in the ornate "red" conference room (red, for some reason, being the official senate color), began without incident. I sat in what had already become my normal seat—in the middle of a sofa against the wall facing the long conference table in the middle of the room. Thirty-five Republican senators and assorted senior staff—about fifty of us in all—milled around, waiting.

Senator Marino took his place at the head of the conference table. He didn't sit but began talking in the distinctive voice that earned him the nickname "Mumbles" among all those associated with state government. "It looks as if we have a deal," he mumbled. Some senators cheered; others clapped. At last, the budget "battle" could come to an end. Marino continued, turning to the top staff member of the Senate Finance Committee, "Please brief the conference."

The staff member outlined the broad parameters of the $64 billion budget deal. It was the first we were hearing of what was in the budget itself. Up until this time, we had heard only what Cuomo would *not* do. We listened attentively, but it was difficult to understand the deal; it was remarkably short on detail and long on generalities.

"How much does this increase spending over last year?" Senator Joe Bruno of Troy asked from his lonely seat near the door at the rear of the conference room.

"We really don't have the numbers yet, Senator," came the staffer's reply.

"What do you mean?" Bruno asked, his voice rising. "I thought there was a deal."

"We really don't have the total yet. I can get you that number, Senator."

"How the hell can we have a budget if we don't even know what we're spending?" Bruno demanded. His face was starting to turn red.

Other senators looked down, or away; some rolled their eyes; some were outraged that Bruno could ask such a question and still get a nonanswer at such a critical time. It was the same question he'd been asking for three weeks, and it was the same answer each time. "I'll get you that information, Senator." "We really don't have those numbers yet, Senator." "I can put something together and get back to you, Senator."

"Is my motor vehicles office still going to be closed?" another senator asked.

"No," he was assured. "We got that in for you."

The senator sat down, relieved.

"How much more does this budget spend than Cuomo proposed in January?" asked Senator Tom Libous of Binghamton, with a frustration to match Bruno's.

"I'll have to get that number for you, Senator," the staffer replied, "but we did get $200 million more for schools."

"That special ed program?" another senator wondered. "Is it still being cut?"

"No," he answered proudly. "We got that in too."

"What about tax cuts?" tried John DeFrancisco, a freshman senator from Syracuse who hadn't yet learned not to ask such questions.

"Well, you know Cuomo. To restore the spending we had to agree to defer the tax cuts again. But we kept them in the law."

Big deal, I thought to myself. How silly is that? Every year, temporary taxes that were meant to expire were extended, while tax cuts that were meant to take effect were delayed. In my view, keeping the cuts on the books with no intention of ever making them happen was dishonest.

"How can we pass a budget with no tax cuts?" DeFrancisco bellowed. "What about temporary taxes?"

"They're still in there," came the subdued reply.

"How can we do this?" Bruno yelled. "How can we agree to this?" He was on his feet again. "Every year we spend more; we tax more. It's just wrong."

Bruno, of course, was right. The acquiescence of senate Republicans on spending and taxes had given New Yorkers the highest tax burden and the worst job record in the United States. The following year, in the gubernatorial campaign, I could honestly travel the state and claim that in New York, Cuomo's temporary taxes had lasted longer than many people's permanent jobs—and it was more than idle rhetoric.

"How much more are we spending?" Bruno railed. He was red-hot now. "How long are we going to buy into this crap?"

At this point, Marino rose to his feet. He didn't like the way things were going. The heated conference—all ten minutes of it—was getting too confrontational for a man who preferred to do his clashing behind closed doors. While the vast majority of the senators in the red conference room had remained silent, and some had been shortsightedly appreciative of certain restorations to the budget, this type of questioning from people like Bruno, DeFrancisco, Libous, and others, like Senator John Daly, could not be allowed to continue.

"We all know how hard we're fighting and how long we've delayed the budget," he finally said. "Cuomo has given in on most of our restorations, and this is a good budget. I've held him up now for weeks. This is the best we can do. We're going to start passing the budget bills this evening."

Bruno wasn't satisfied by Marino's attempt to calm him down, and I couldn't blame him. It was clear he'd been cut off. It was time to move from the mere details of $64 billion in spending and on to the logistics of passing the bills.

"I expect all of us to vote for the budget," Marino insisted, "and against any amendments the Democrats might offer." He said this with the full confidence of a man whose wishes had rarely been ignored.

I raised my hand, and Marino did not look pleased to see it. "Senator," I said, trying not to let my anger show, "I can't vote for this budget." My blood pressure must have been over 200, but I kept on. "I ran for office believing we must cut spending and taxes, and I won't vote for a budget that doesn't accomplish that."

It was as though a skunk had just let loose. The level of discomfort and tension shot up beyond the level of tolerance. Since January, Republican senators had been quietly assessing my arrival in their ranks, wondering if I'd turn out to be a team player or a Benedict Arnold. Now they had their answer.

Senator Marino retained his composure. "The conference is over," he announced. "Let's go right to the chamber to start voting." He banged his gavel to dismiss the caucus, and then he turned to me. "George," he said, "I'll see you in my office."

I'll see you in my office. It was like being in school again and summoned to see the principal. Taken to the woodshed for a choice between potential pain or political gain. It had worked every time for the past fifteen years.

Not this time.

That night, the first three budget bills were passed, the Republican majority all but united in its common front and praising another "excellent budget" that would do so much for the people of New York State. Joe Bruno said nothing, but his red face let everyone know his true feelings. I was taken to Marino's woodshed, but I voted "no" anyway. Another Republican conference was called for ten o'clock the next morning, and I went out into the night to lick my wounds and consider my options.

Mike Finnegan and I went out to McGeary's, one of Albany's great Irish watering holes. Normally, after a late session such as this one, I'd go out for a hamburger and beer with a half-dozen of my new senate colleagues, but not tonight. They didn't want me along with them, and I didn't particularly want their company either. So it was Finnegan and I.

"Well, what do you think?" I asked Mike. Finnegan had been my friend, counsel, neighbor, and coconspirator in Peekskill since we had recrossed paths during a gubernatorial campaign ten years earlier. I trusted his judgment.

"Tough, real tough," Mike replied, shaking his head. "But it had to be done."

"Another round?" our waiter asked.

Tonight, the answer was easy.

"And tomorrow?" I said to Mike. "That's when we have all the major budget bills. You know Marino was tough on me in there. I've got to vote no, but it's all over for me in the senate."

"What's the choice? You ran saying you would cut taxes. You ran saying the Republican senate was part of the problem. You said you'd be different."

He was right. I did. I had no choice but to vote no. "Yeah," I said, "there goes my career in the senate."

"What can they do to you? We had nothing in the assembly. No staff. No member items. No bills. And still we made a difference. You're the first one in twenty years to do the right thing. It'll all work out."

This last wasn't said with a great deal of conviction, but I chose to take Mike at his word. For twenty years, since I started out as a staffer for Peekskill's state senator, Bernie Gordon, my dream had been to make it to the state senate. Now, here I was, and my dream was turning into a nightmare.

It would have been amusing if it hadn't been so brutal, and so totally unexpected. In truth, all I was doing was what the rest of these people should have been doing all along: standing up for what's right and representing the interests of the people. I was holding out against the tide, shoring up the walls of my fort, beating back the inevitable waves. I was doing my job.

The most galling factor was that for all the ranting and railing, the apparent consequences of my vote didn't amount to much: The budget simply passed by a slightly smaller margin. But what really happened was far more dramatic. My actions posed a threat to the way things were done on Marino's watch, and they set me apart as a pariah. Most Republican senators knew that what they were doing was wrong, they were good people who essentially shared my convictions, but they were unwilling to take the heat alone. Now, with my vote, they could be challenged by their constituents: "Pataki voted no. Why not you?" It was a question they didn't want to hear, let alone have to answer.

I knew the party leaders would try to punish me for my defiance, in the petty way that had for too long marked our state government. As a freshman senator, I had achieved only one provision in the budget that first year—payment of taxes on state parkland in my district in Putnam County. It was a small thing, but it meant the world at home. There are sixty-two counties in the state of New York, many of which received payments, usually based on the political clout of their legislators. Putnam County never received a dime. For too long, we'd been left off the ledger, but with my passion for acquiring open-space parkland, and for lower property taxes, I could not let that situation stand. I had sought this measure to change our status. It was more than just unfair, it was also costly for my constituents. But Governor Cuomo used his line-item veto to kill the provision. In fact, he line-itemed only two provisions in the entire budget that year—a small appropriation for the chairman of the Senate Finance Committee, and my measure for Putnam County—and I had no doubt that he did so to pay me back for my "no" vote on the overall budget, and at the request of his partner in government, Ralph Marino.

I called him on it. "Governor," I said, at my first opportunity, "why are you doing this?"

His response was coolly typical: "How many people live in Putnam County?"

"Forgive me, Governor," I said, as respectfully as I could manage, "but that's not the basis on which to make a policy decision. How many people live in the county? Why is that even relevant? It shouldn't matter how many people live in the county. All these other counties have this provision. It's the right thing to do."

With this he backed off a little bit. "Well," he finally said, "what you're looking for is a permanent change. It's not a budget item. It shouldn't be in the budget."

With a stroke of his pen, he saw that it wasn't, but there was more to it than that. I knew as surely as the tide would eventually come in that Cuomo took a call from Ralph Marino at some eleventh hour, during which the senate majority leader told the governor that I was opposing his budget and suggested he veto my provision to teach me a lesson. Naturally, it wouldn't have looked right to veto just one provision, so they hit on the appropriations item, most likely thinking that the chairman of the Senate Finance Committee had so much else going on in the budget that he wouldn't mind losing out on this one article.

That's the way the game was played, and here again it bothered the hell out of me that it was even considered a game. It made my skin crawl that this was what our state government had been reduced to, and I wasn't playing. I vowed to finish out my term and move on—not because I wasn't up to the fight, but because I realized that under their leadership at that time, the senate Republicans were a substantial part of the problem and there was no changing the fabric, not while Ralph Marino was the leader.

Looking back later on that experience I wondered: As governor, would I be able to make a real difference? After all, look what I'd be dealing with: a Democratic assembly that was eager not just to preserve, but to advance the failed, misguided policies that were bankrupting New York's future and a senate majority leader who had helped the assemblymen to do it—a man who had forfeited principle for political expediency and, worse, prevented his members from voting as their conscience directed.

Fortunately, this dreadful scenario never had the chance to materialize. After my election, Marino was ousted as majority leader and replaced by Joe Bruno, whose conservative beliefs are strong, genuine, and deeply rooted in lifelong convictions. I put together the most principled, loyal, and hardworking staff a governor could ever hope for: men and women who love New York as much as I do, and share my vision of leading our state along the path to its true destiny of unmatched greatness and limitless opportunity.

It soon became clear that as governor I *was* going to make a difference—and in more ways than one. I began to realize that even in my darkest moments on the job I could somehow bring light to someone, somewhere.

Ironically, this realization came during the saddest time of my term in office: the evening of July 17, 1996, when TWA Flight 800 crashed off the coast of Long Island.

When I heard the news, everything that had seemed important just minutes before suddenly became irrelevant. And reflecting on it now, I know that one of the most important functions a governor can fulfill is to extend a caring hand to people in despair and give them what they need most in times of sorrow: comfort, understanding, and a shoulder to cry on.

Because the tragedy had occurred ten miles offshore, and because the recovery effort was taking so long, the shock and sorrow that family members were experiencing was compounded by the fact that they were in a strange and unfamiliar place. They didn't know where to go or who to turn to. The recovery effort seemed endless, and there were no answers. The confusion seemed only to intensify their despair. We had to bring them together, in one place, where they could join hands and turn to one another for support.

So, days after the disaster, I held a memorial service on the beach closest to the site of the crash. The service was broadcast worldwide, enabling people everywhere to join in the mourning and to show love and support for the family members who needed it so desperately. I ended the service by telling the family members: "Long after this horrible tragedy, and long after those who are assembled here have dispersed, we will be thinking of you."

I have never stopped thinking of them. The moments I spent with them are forever etched in my mind and in my heart. Many of them told me that the service and all of the state's efforts in their behalf had helped to ease their pain. What this means to me I cannot possibly express in words.

On the first anniversary of the tragedy, we returned to that beach on Long Island. Hundreds of family members were there. And although our reunion was a solemn one—born of tragedy—I knew we had shared something deeply personal that could never be taken away.

On that day, I knew that the beach would always be a sacred place for the family members, and that a piece of their hearts would always be there. The media covering the service spoke of this as being a time of closure. But I knew that for many of the loved ones, there would be no closure. At least, not on this day. As the loving parent of four, I wanted them to know that I understood, in my comments to the crowd.

"You are like the mother who sacrifices all she has—moving heaven and earth—to protect her child from the inevitable dangers of life. From birth, she takes every care and caution in the world, pampering her child with the utmost care and tenderest hands. She's there to guide every step, break every fall, dry every tear.

There is no sadness so great as when, despite all her efforts, all her precautions and all her love, there is nothing more a mother can do to protect her child.

To all of the mothers and fathers, sisters and brothers, sons and daughters . . . To all of you who lost the ones you loved, protected, and cared for most . . . To all of you who still struggle with feelings of helplessness and despair . . .

. . . Just as a child has unconditional faith in the loving hands of his mother, have faith that the ones you mourn are safe in the loving hands of God."

That beach where the families of Flight 800 left flowers for their loved ones wasn't far from the beach where we had built walls against the tide as kids. It wasn't far from where Libby and I had collided twenty-five years earlier. It wasn't far from where the kids and I had built walls in our own competition to hold back time and tide.

And that beach makes me think, Yes, it does matter. Yes, government can make a difference, a profound difference, in the lives of millions. It can relieve a bit of the anguish for a visitor from France over the loss of his sister. It can ease the fears of a mother in Harlem as she sees her daughter off to school on a September morning. It can end the fear of a retired couple in Buffalo that they can't pay the school taxes on the house they've worked for, lived in, and raised a family in. It can provide hope, in the form of a job, for a former welfare recipient in Elmira. And it can offer opportunity, the opportunity to see the American dream be alive and well for an immigrant family newly arrived in Queens who hope someday their grandchild can be governor or president.

New York is now leading the nation in all the right categories—leading in reducing violent crime, leading in reducing welfare dependency, leading in cutting taxes, leading in providing clean air and water and economic opportunities. The tides of decline and despair are in retreat. The walls we are building on a strong foundation are getting stronger and higher, and public confidence is growing.

Policy does make a difference. Vision and content do matter. The New York of 1998 is as vibrant, open, optimistic, and confident as the New York of 1898. The twenty-first century will see heights of opportunity and achievement unimaginable in the twentieth century.

As I crossed the state in 1994, I had ended my appearances with this comment: "Libby and I have four kids. Soon they'll all be off in college. When they're finished, they will have a choice to settle anywhere in America. I don't want to have to visit them in Atlanta, or Dallas, or Durham, because they've gone there seeking to build their futures and families elsewhere. I want to be able to visit them down the street, right here in New York State."

A little over a year after that morning on the beach in 1996, Emily began her freshman year at Yale College, in New Haven, Connecticut. As Libby and I and her brothers and sister left Emily's dorm room, I had mixed emotions. I was sad that she was leaving home and going away to school. I was pleased, though, that she was entering the great school that her father, uncle, and grandfather had attended. I was sad she was leaving New York State, but pleased because I knew that when she was through with college, after receiving one of the best educations possible in America—or maybe the world—she would come back to New York to pursue her version of the American dream for herself and for her family. New York had become again a place of excitement, a place of opportunity, the place where dreams come true. We had not been futilely building walls against the tide. We had not been engaged in a meaningless game. We had changed the rules, changed the future. The tomatoes planted in April were bearing fruit. The journey up the Hudson Valley, from Ellis Island to Peekskill to Albany, had meant everything.

Index